HOW TO HELP SOMEONE WITH DEPRESSION

TRIGGER™

The mental health & wellbeing publisher

ABOUT THE AUTHOR

Dr Emma Cotterill is a clinical psychologist experienced in supporting people with a range of mental health difficulties, including depression. She also works in neuropsychology, supporting those who have sustained life-changing brain injuries. Alongside individual psychological therapy work, Emma is a trainer, writer and supervisor, and is passionate about mental health education and supporting wellbeing.

She lives in Surrey, where she is a parent and enjoys fitness, reading, music and paddle boarding. You can read more about Emma and her work here: www.empowerpsychology.co.uk

HOW TO HELP SOMEONE WITH DEPRESSION

A Practical Toolkit

Dr Emma Cotterill

TRIGGER™
The mental health & wellbeing publisher

This edition published in 2023 by Trigger Publishing
An imprint of Shaw Callaghan Ltd

UK Office
The Stanley Building
7 Pancras Square
Kings Cross
London N1C 4AG

US Office
On Point Executive Center, Inc
3030 N Rocky Point Drive W
Suite 150
Tampa, FL 33607
www.triggerhub.org

A CIP catalogue record for this book is available upon request from the British Library
ISBN: 978-1-83796-262-4
Ebook ISBN: 978-1-83796-263-1

Typeset by Lapiz Digital Services

This book is dedicated to every person supporting someone with depression right now.

CONTENTS

INTRODUCTION

If you are reading this, it is likely that depression has touched your life in some way. You may be looking to learn more about supporting a person with depression for yourself, or on behalf of others. You may know someone who is experiencing depression now or who has done so in the past. You may be struggling yourself. You may be worried, sad, stressed, frustrated, overwhelmed. You may be feeling unsure, at a loss, worn out, confused, angry, guilty, hopeless. It is understandable to have all these feelings and more.

You are likely here because you want to help. Because you want to understand. Because you need hope. Because you need to find the light not only for the person with depression, but for yourself too.

Supporting a person with depression can be really tough. Throughout this journey, it is important to be kind to yourself. Then be even kinder.

"You are likely here because you need hope. Because you need to find the light not only for the person with depression, but for yourself too."

ABOUT ME

As a clinical psychologist, I'm passionate about psychology and providing therapeutic services to help people. I'm also a parent, friend, daughter, sibling, partner and colleague. I know how difficult it can be to see someone you care about overcome with the darkness, loneliness and heaviness of depression. I understand how hard it can feel when supporting someone with depression, how you can worry about doing or saying the right thing, and at times feel exhausted or worn down by it all.

I am grateful for the experiences that have helped me understand depression from many different perspectives, and I am honoured and privileged to have been able to sit alongside my clients, friends, colleagues and loved ones as they have talked about their experiences with depression and to have been able to support them along their journey.

HOW THIS BOOK WORKS

This book is written for you, so that you can have a better understanding of depression and how to help. It is divided into two parts:

In Part 1 you will build up your understanding of depression – the signs and symptoms; what can lead to a person experiencing depression; and what the experience can be like.

Part 2 focuses on your supporting role – what to say, what to do, and how. And also what not to say and do. We will explore the core skills, strategies and approaches you can draw on to support a person with depression, giving you the tools to respond to the challenges the depression brings.

As you reach the end of the book, you will learn about the professional support available for the person you are helping, as well as how to take care of yourself.

"I would like to invite you to create a toolkit for yourself of knowledge, understanding, skills, strategies, self-care and resources, which will help you understand and support the person with depression as best you can, whilst maintaining your own self-care and boundaries."

THE SUPPORTER'S TOOLKIT

As you read this book, I would like to invite you to create a toolkit for yourself of knowledge, understanding, skills, strategies, self-care and resources, which will help you understand and support the person with depression as best you can, whilst maintaining your own self-care and boundaries.

Throughout each chapter, we will add to your toolkit, which will include:

- Developing a knowledge of depression
- Understanding the lived experience of depression
- Understanding what you bring to the situation as a supporter, with your own thoughts, feelings, experiences, coping styles and expectations
- Practical ways you can help and support – what you can say and do
- Where to find support for the person with depression.
- How you can look after yourself, so you can be the most effective supporter you can be
- A library of resources, and further reading should you want to explore further

As you work through this book, and build your toolkit, I would encourage you to highlight parts of the book to help you remember and find key points at a later date.

TERMINOLOGY

The person you are supporting could be your friend, family member, partner, neighbour, colleague, employee, or someone else you have a relationship with. You may be very close, or you may be an acquaintance who cares. To capture the range of these relationships and the experience of living with depression I will talk about 'the person with depression' throughout.

Amongst people who experience depression, there is a range of words that people use to describe their experience. Some people talk about their depression as an experience, some talk about it as a mental health condition, problem, or as an illness or ill health. Throughout this book I will mostly refer to the experience of depression as a mental health condition. However, you, and the person with depression may feel more comfortable with one description over another, and that is OK.

SHARED STORIES

To help understand depression fully, I have shared words and stories from some incredible people who have experienced depression, and who have kindly contributed to this book. I am grateful to every person who has shared their words to help us understand depression from their lived experience. I hope you find these stories as helpful and inspiring as I did when listening to them.

I hope that this book will be useful, positive, uplifting and inspiring for you, providing you with the ideas, tools and strategies to help someone who is struggling right now.

PART 1

UNDERSTANDING DEPRESSION

CHAPTER 1

WHAT IS DEPRESSION?

Depression. It's likely you've heard this word, spoken it, and worried about it many times before you've opened this book. You might be tired of hearing it, of seeing its impact on your life, and on the life of people you know, love or care about. It might feel like a really heavy, scary word. So, the first thing I'd like to do is explain it, to help you understand what 'depression' means. Because understanding is the first step in helping someone with depression to move out of the darkness into the light. I hope it will also help you feel less in the dark too.

WHAT IS MEANT BY DEPRESSION?

Depression is a grey sky when everyone tells you there is light. It is feeling too much or feeling nothing at all. It is finding a way through each day despite the pain, the aches, the fatigue. It is silently crumbling whilst outwardly smiling. It is feeling lost and alone in the middle of a sea of people. It is an unwanted visitor. An invisible uninvited silent companion.

Depression is an extremely common mental health condition that affects:

- How a person thinks, feels and behaves
- How they sleep, eat, move and communicate
- Their view of themselves and their relationships
- Their ability to engage with activities and social groups that they may have previously enjoyed
- Their ability to see a hopeful future, to enjoy the present, or to move forward from the past

Anyone can experience depression. Depression does not discriminate. Depression can impact people of any age, gender, sexuality, ethnicity, culture, religion, class, financial status and job status.

Depression is not just 'sadness' – this is a common misconception – it is far, far more than this. And it is not just a fleeting moment, a few hours or days; it is an ongoing state, in which depression creeps slowly and quietly into daily life.

This misconception may be exacerbated by people saying they 'feel depressed' when they are a bit down or fed up. All of us get sad or fed up at times; we might want to cry, or not get out of bed. This is all part of the normal human experience. However, there is a difference between feeling low for a few days, compared to weeks or months. When a person begins feeling any of the symptoms of depression, over two weeks or more, with a negative impact on their quality of life, then you know it is something very different to 'just having a bad day'.

THE STATS

At the time of writing, the World Health Organization (WHO) describes the prevalence of depression as affecting more than 264 million people worldwide. If we imagine that each of these people has at least one friend and one family member supporting them, then that is at least 528 million people, just like yourself, trying to do their best, trying to make sense of what depression is and trying to understand how they can help. Figures like these help us understand how very common depression is.

THE SYMPTOMS OF DEPRESSION

There are a number of common symptoms of depression. However, every person's experience of depression will be individual, so not everyone will have all the symptoms identified here.

EMOTIONS (MOODS/FEELINGS)

- Sadness
- Unhappiness
- Grief/loss
- Loneliness (even in company)
- Anxiety/worry/panic
- Irritability
- Frustration
- Anger
- Despair
- Guilt
- Shame
- Loss of pleasure in activities
- Numbness
- Hopelessness

COGNITIVE SYMPTOMS (THOUGHTS AND THINKING PROCESSES)

- Self-critical thoughts and beliefs: for example, 'I am not good enough'/'I am a failure'/'I am useless'/'I don't get anything right'/'I am worthless'
- Negative thoughts/beliefs about others and the world: for example, 'The world is unsafe'/'People are not trustworthy'/'Everyone else is better than me'

- Negative perspectives and assumptions: for example, catastrophizing/assuming others will be thinking the worst of you/focusing on the worst-case scenario/being caught up in negative 'what ifs'
- Rigid rules about how to live life; expectations of how life 'should'/'must'/'ought' to be
- Dwelling on memories of past failures or expected future ones
- Thoughts about the future that centre on a sense of hopelessness and meaninglessness
- Thoughts of self-harm and/or suicidal ideation
- Difficulty paying attention/concentrating
- Difficulty remembering new information – short-term memory concerns
- Difficulty making decisions or problem-solving
- Slowed-down thinking – feeling in a fog, taking longer to process information

PHYSICAL SYMPTOMS
- Lethargy/fatigue
- Body aches and pains, such as headaches, shoulder tension or tight chest
- Loss of appetite or craving foods (particularly sugary foods) leading to overeating or undereating
- Loss of energy and motivation

- Sleep changes – difficulties in getting to sleep, waking during the night/insomnia or early-morning waking

BEHAVIOURAL SYMPTOMS

- Withdrawal and avoidance of people, social situations, work, relationships and leisure activities
- Rumination – constantly focusing on negative thoughts with repetitive worries
- Increase in use of drugs/alcohol
- Restlessness/agitation
- Neglect of self-care/personal care
- Self-harm*
- Suicidal plans and behaviours*

* I know that talking about self-harm and suicide can feel very difficult. Take a breath and give yourself a moment if you need to. We will talk about how to understand and support this in Chapter 4.

THE DEPRESSION SPECTRUM

Understanding depression along a spectrum or continuum can be helpful to capture the wide range of individual experiences. It can be useful to understand that people can have experiences ranging from 'not depressed', to experiencing some minor symptoms, to having some severe symptoms, to being severely depressed. The person may move back and forward along the depression spectrum throughout their journey with depression, and this might fluctuate over hours, days, weeks, with some moments seeming lighter and others feeling much, much heavier.

The idea of a depression spectrum can be helpful for people who may wonder if they are depressed, but because they have good days, or good moments, they think they can't be. It can also help you notice and understand the fluctuating symptoms in the person you care about where their symptoms may appear lighter and milder one day, and then heavier the next. Within the spectrum, there is space for any individual experiences to find a place that we can understand as experiences of depression. We can then find ways to provide help and support, and the person themselves can find ways to help and support themselves to move along the spectrum toward 'not depressed'.

IDENTIFYING DEPRESSION

There are different routes to identifying if depression is present. You could support the person experiencing depression to consider any of the following (or all three if they choose):

1. **Seek a formal diagnosis:** A medical or health professional can complete an assessment to confirm if depression is present. This may be through a formal diagnosis using a set criteria (see below). In addition, some other health professionals such as clinical psychologists also use a process called formulation, which involves collaboratively drawing up a shared understanding of a person's experiences that have led to and may be maintaining the presence of depression. This may involve acknowledging if a person's experiences fit within the spectrum of depression. The British Psychological Society recently published a report on depression in 2020 that explains this further.[1] They also published a document with the Division of Clinical Psychology on understanding psychiatric diagnosis which you may also find helpful.[2]

2. **Complete a self-report questionnaire:** This identifies common symptoms of depression. There are a number of self-report questionnaires some of which are freely available on the internet (see Resources at the back of this book); one example is the Patient Health Questionnaire (PHQ-9).

3. **Psychoeducate:** Read information about depression symptoms and experiences from reliable sources to see if these fit with the person's experiences.

IS A DIAGNOSIS NECESSARY?

The answer is: maybe. Many people with depression seek a diagnosis and benefit from it, and equally there are people who never receive a formal diagnosis, who are still experiencing depression and who will benefit from support.

The person you are supporting with depression right now may have their own views on whether they want or need a diagnosis. It is not compulsory or always necessary. Depression doesn't need a diagnosis to exist and there are many routes to understanding depression and finding a way out of it that do not all require this professional intervention. Without a diagnosis you can still understand that symptoms of depression are present, that a person's depression exists along a continuum, and you can still help and support them to engage in interventions and strategies for overcoming the symptoms they are experiencing.

Of course, at times, it is very helpful to seek a diagnosis. The advantages may include the person finding comfort in 'knowing' what they are experiencing, and being able to give it a name and share this with others. A diagnosis can be useful on a practical level to help someone qualify for time off or sick pay, and access therapy or medication that require a diagnosis as part of the process.

UNDERSTANDING DIAGNOSIS IN DEPRESSION

Clinically, there are two key diagnostic classification systems used worldwide: the *Diagnostic and Statistical Manual of Mental Disorders* (DSM-IV), published by the American Psychiatric Association and the *International Classification of Diseases and Related Health Problems* (ICD-10), published by the World Health Organization.

Each classification system sets out depression-related diagnoses (each has more than one potential diagnosis), and the signs and symptoms required for a formal diagnosis. A diagnosis typically requires symptoms to be ongoing for over two weeks.

A health or medical professional will talk to the person with depression, and ask questions to find out if they are experiencing symptoms that meet the diagnostic criteria.

I have summarized the common depression-related diagnoses that we typically see under the umbrella of depression. However, this isn't an exhaustive list and the ICD-10 and DSM-IV have several different diagnoses that clinicians may use.

Major depressive episode: This is the most common depression diagnosis, also referred to as clinical depression. It can be classed as mild, moderate or severe depending on the severity of the symptoms and the impact on day-to-day functioning.

Depression with psychotic features: A person can experience depression with psychosis, which includes features such as hallucinations or delusions.

Dysthymia: A person may experience fewer depression symptoms, below the severity required for clinical depression, but these symptoms exist for two years or more.

Postnatal depression or post-partum depression (PND/PPD): PND/PPD involves experiencing symptoms of depression after having a baby. Statistics suggest this affects 10–15 per cent of women, or possibly 3 in 10 women, as these figures may be under reported due to lack of disclosure to health professionals. It is also important to highlight that PND/PPD also affects 10 per cent of new fathers. In addition, perinatal depression is when it is experienced prior to the baby being born, when the mother or father may experience depression during the pregnancy.

Seasonal affective disorder (SAD): SAD affects people in a seasonal pattern, particularly within the winter months.

Bipolar affective disorder: Commonly referred to as bipolar disorder, or previously, manic depression, this is considered a severe and lifelong mental illness, typically diagnosed from 18 years old onward. It is characterized by periods of depression and periods of mania (elevated mood/thoughts and activity levels). Bipolar disorder can and should be understood very separately to depression, although depression of course is part of the overall picture of this illness.

As with the depression spectrum, it is helpful to understand that a diagnosis of depression is not a fixed state. It can and will change. A mild depression may become severe, a severe depression may become moderate, and a person may recover entirely.

Please note: In this book we will focus on depression as an overall condition, rather than a specific diagnosis. If you want to read more about these specific conditions, see Resources at the back of the book.

HOW LONG DOES DEPRESSION LAST?

How long a period of depression lasts can be different for each person. It may be:

- Several weeks or months
- A single episode or two or more (repeated) episodes during the course of their life, with periods when they do not feel depressed in between
- Ongoing symptoms of depression over a much longer period of time (years), with only mild fluctuations

There is no standard length of an episode of depression. It may vary for many reasons and it is why it is important to gently let go of our expectations of when a person 'should' get better.

"Learning to live in a more meaningful way – albeit alongside or in spite of the depression – is always possible."

It can be tough to accept that for some people depression may always be a part of their lives, albeit with periods (sometimes very long periods) of respite when the depression may be quieter or disappear. This can be difficult to think about if you are close to someone. However, knowing that depression may be in a person's life for longer than hoped or wished for does not mean that the experience of depression cannot change, or how it is managed cannot change. Learning to live in a more meaningful way – albeit alongside or in spite of the depression – is always possible.

DEPRESSION AND DIVERSITY

The experience of depression can increase or show up in different ways for different groups of people. For example:

- Depression in younger people may be missed as it might look like normal childhood behaviours or emotional turmoil. You might notice they refuse to go to school, have poor sleep and/or poor concentration, talk negatively about themselves, and cry or be angrier than usual.

- Older people with depression may express physical concerns, rather than any negative emotions, and they may report sleeping problems, irritability and being less focused. They may have grown up in a society or culture that did not accept talking about mental health difficulties and may be more reluctant to consider talking about how they are feeling.

- Depression in men can sometimes look like anger, aggression and irritability. They may be more likely to talk about physical aches and pains, such as headaches and stomach issues. They may struggle with sleep issues and may try to cope through using drugs or alcohol. Concerns about substance use may then become the focus, rather than the underlying depression.

- Men who are experiencing depression are also at high risk of suicidal thoughts and behaviours. Mental health charity CALM (Campaign Against Living Miserably) report that in the UK 75 per cent of suicides are men.[3] According to the UK's Office of National Statistics, males aged 45-49 are at the highest risk.[4] I know reading this might be really scary if you know someone in this group suffering with depression right now. Remember, there is help and support. See Chapter 4 for how to support risk and Chapter 11 for accessing professional support.

- Higher levels of depression have been found within the LGBTQ+ community. Struggles with acceptance, ill treatment and discrimination can all be part of why this community may be more vulnerable to depression.
- People with a learning disability can have a higher incidence of depression than the general population. They can struggle to be properly heard and listened to if their mental health is suffering. For some people with learning disabilities, there may be an increase in challenging behaviour as they struggle to express how they feel.
- Depression has been found to be misunderstood or misdiagnosed within the black community and other ethnic minority groups. Depression can present differently or with subtle differences within different ethnic groups, which can lead to it being missed or misunderstood if health professionals are not trained to be racially or culturally sensitive and thoughtful in their work.
- Racism can also play a role in the ability of people with depression to feel heard, appropriately supported and access racially sensitive interventions. Racism and oppression are also, of course, a large cause of depression within these communities. Without question, there is significant work to be done to increase awareness, education and understanding, and to improve services and professional training. These are needed to address

systemic issues of racism and related ethnicity and cultural issues within mental health services. It is beyond the scope of this book to address this in more detail, however please see Resources for further reading.

- Stigma and shame can also be attached to depression and can lead people to conceal their symptoms or to stop people understanding, recognizing and seeking help for depression.

Depression creeps into a person's life, often slowly, insidiously. It distorts their thoughts, like an all-encompassing negative filter through which every thought flows. It steals their sleep, leaving them awake and alone in the darkest moments of the night. It can grip a person with despair, anxiety, panic. It slows them down. Their body aches. Thinking is foggy. It tells a person that they are no good. It throws them waves of hopelessness. It sneaks away their appetite or urges them to overeat, or drink or smoke, to numb, escape, avoid. It is a constant persuasive companion, but it is not a friend.

CHAPTER 2

WHY DO PEOPLE EXPERIENCE DEPRESSION?

A common question is: 'Why is the person I am supporting depressed?' It can often feel frustrating and puzzling, especially if there is no obvious reason from your perspective. Yet the reality is that there are many reasons which on their own, or in combination, can have an impact on a person developing and maintaining depression, which we will explore in this chapter.

Sometimes a person may struggle to identify why they are feeling depressed, which can increase their distress, leaving them feeling even more of a failure. There are different ways to make sense of this struggle. This may be because the depression has more of a biological/genetic component (see page 26); it may be because the depression makes the person minimize their stressors and traumas and so may conclude they have no good reason to feel depressed; or they may not be fully aware of the complex interaction of potential causes/contributing factors (as set out below) that can lead to depression.

"Sometimes a person may struggle to identify why they are feeling depressed, which can increase their distress."

UNDERSTANDING THE 'WHY'

People who experience depression may be affected by one or more of the areas listed below. Often, they interact to influence why a person starts experiencing depression and why depression continues over time.

- Childhood experiences
- Family dynamics
- Life stressors (current/past stressors)
- Biology/genetics
- Brain chemistry/hormones
- Relationship patterns
- Trauma
- Physical health

- Belief about self/world/others
- Resources/coping strategies
- Level of support

A NOTE ABOUT PRIVILEGE

There are so many areas of life experience (e.g. childhood, adult life and internal functioning), that can lead to depression, regardless of how wonderful things may look from the outside. It is really important to keep in mind that a person can be living a seemingly fortunate or privileged life and still have depression. They may have, for example, a lovely family, support network and financial security. If they then experience depression, their external privilege can exacerbate their suffering as they criticize themselves further for feeling depressed.

CHILDHOOD EXPERIENCES

What we experience in childhood influences how we view ourselves, others and the world around us. Our upbringing can begin to determine if we feel safe, if we see ourselves as a good enough person or if we trust others. It can determine how we learn to cope, how we react when under stress, how we think about mental health, and much more. Research has identified adverse childhood experiences (ACEs) that have been linked to problems in later life, for example:

- Physical abuse
- Sexual abuse
- Emotional abuse
- Neglect
- Domestic violence in the home
- A family member in prison
- Separation or divorce
- Substance misuse in the family
- Serious mental ill health in the family

Family dynamics may also play a part. Relationships with your primary caregiver (the main adult looking after you and responsible for keeping you safe) is often relevant. Attachment theory explains how the connections and attachments we form with our primary caregiver can create a relationship imprint that can repeat throughout our life. Other relationships within the household may also be important in determining how we learn to trust and feel safe with others.

People may have tried to move on from their childhood experiences, but early trauma, whether at home or in school (e.g. bullying, experiences of anger/aggression, or physical/

emotional/sexual abuse or neglect) can have long-lasting impacts far beyond childhood.

Growing up in a stressful family environment where any of the following are present can also have an impact on longer-term coping and mental health: financial or work stresses, poverty, discrimination, relationship breakdowns, unhelpful or unhealthy parental coping strategies and poor mental health in the family.

LIFE STRESSORS

Experiencing stressful events, at any time in life, can lead to depression. These might be one-off events or multiple events at the same time or over time. These events might not *appear* stressful, or even that big of a deal from the outside, but keep in mind that what a person finds stressful is unique to them. It is how *they perceive and experience* the stressful event that is important, not how we or others may perceive or experience it.

> "It is how a person perceives and experiences the stressful event that is important, not how we or others may perceive or experience it."

Life stressors may include any of the following:

- Loss of job/redundancy
- Financial stress/losses
- Loss of loved one
- Breakdown of relationship/divorce
- Assault
- Moving house
- Bullying
- Social stressors/social media
- Injury/illness – related to self or loved one
- Infertility issues
- Disability
- Retirement
- Pregnancy
- Making sense of sexuality/sexual identity
- Experiencing racism/sexism/prejudice/discrimination
- Parenting/child-related worries/stresses
- Living in a pandemic

TRAUMATIC EXPERIENCES

Experiencing a trauma can lead to a very specific set of symptoms and mental health difficulties known as post-traumatic stress disorder (PTSD). The person may also develop depression alongside PTSD, or develop depression following the trauma, but without a diagnosis of PTSD.

The timeline between when a trauma was experienced and being depressed can vary. It may develop years after the trauma occurred, possibly triggered by a more recent stressful event.

Traumatic events may be 'big' single-incident traumas (e.g. a car accident, abuse, assault) or seemingly 'smaller' events that have a 'drip-drip' effect, from living with a problematic situation over time. Examples might include bullying in the workplace or at school, living with a highly critical/emotional neglecting partner/parent, walking on eggshells around an angry parent, growing up feeling neglected or lonely. In addition, a childhood experience, however small, that was frightening or overwhelming, and still resonates many years on, can be a trauma.

SELF-ESTEEM AND SELF-BELIEF

People who have developed low self-esteem and/or hold negative beliefs about themselves, developed through their early life experiences (e.g. 'I'm not good enough'/'I'm a failure'/'I'm useless'/'Everyone else is better than me') may be vulnerable to experiencing depression both as a young person or into adulthood. Depression can magnify any existing negative beliefs or thoughts and may spiral these into greater significance.

SUBSTANCE USE

Problematic use of alcohol and drugs can lead to depression. This can also be a vicious cycle where a stressful event leads to depression, so the person uses substances to cope and that gradually becomes problematic, leading to depression.

BIOLOGY, GENETICS AND HEALTH

Research into depression and the brain is ongoing. There is an understanding that some people may have a genetic vulnerability to experiencing depression and there are some signs that there may be an increased risk of depression if an immediate relative has suffered a severe depressive episode.

Scientists are also researching the role of chemicals (known as neurotransmitters) and brain structures in depression. It is known that neurotransmitters such as dopamine and serotonin play a part, and it can be problematic if the amount of neurotransmitter released, or the reception of these neurotransmitters in the brain, does not go smoothly. However depression is not understood to be as simple as being a 'chemical imbalance' and is best understood within the context of all the areas described in this chapter.

Hormones can also play a part. For example, an underactive thyroid (therefore reduced thyroid hormone) can lead to depressive symptoms, as can changes related to menstrual hormones. It is important to ensure these hormonal changes are diagnosed and treated properly in the first instance to clarify if the depression exists alongside these imbalances or whether it gets resolved once the imbalances have been addressed.

"Ultimately, the more healthy, effective coping strategies we have, and the more ability we have to be self-compassionate and look after ourselves at times of stress, the more effective our coping will be."

Lastly, health problems have been known to have an impact on people experiencing depression. For some, depression may be impacted by brain changes as a result of injury or illness (e.g. dementia, traumatic brain injury); whereas for others the depression may be due to the psychological adjustment to a physical illness, injury or health problems.

INEFFECTIVE COPING STRATEGIES

How a person copes with life's challenges can make a difference to how their mental health strengthens or deteriorates. Some coping strategies may work for small difficulties, but not be as effective with larger life stresses. Ultimately, the more healthy, effective coping strategies we have, and the more ability we have to be self-compassionate and look after ourselves at times of stress, the more effective our coping will be. However, unhelpful coping strategies may include:

Ignoring the problem: Trying to not think about something or shutting it out is a common (not often helpful) coping strategy to deal with small day-to-day problems, but using this as a way of dealing with significant life stresses may lead to a person becoming overwhelmed.

Being self-critical: People can develop a strong critical inner voice growing up, which becomes even louder and stronger with stress/depression. The person may feel they deserve the self-criticism or that it helps in some way to motivate them, or that they are just 'being honest with themselves'. Research tells us, however, that self-criticism rarely helps lift our mood or drives us forward in a healthy way.

Using alcohol, drugs or food: Turning to alcohol, drugs or food as a way of coping with difficult feelings, can also impact on a person's mood and ability to cope. It can become problematic if a person who has typically used one or more of these to manage their feelings tries to continue to do so to cope with depression.

AVAILABLE RESOURCES

A person's experience of developing or maintaining depression may be impacted by the resources they have available. Whilst none of these will be a golden ticket to preventing depression, having resources to make life a little easier may help a little. Examples might include:

- Finances to enable someone to access support, take time off work, go for a short break or a holiday, or pay for a relaxing activity
- Access to fitness, such as a gym membership
- A car or affordable transport
- Pleasant places to visit, such as nearby parks
- Being able to access/create and eat nourishing foods
- A comfortable bed/quiet bedroom/own space to rest
- Access to self-help reading materials/the internet to research or find help

Time is often a big resource that is frequently limited. If a person is struggling between working two jobs to pay the bills, being a parent, a partner, a carer, running a house, alongside other life commitments, it can be common for them to not look after themselves. This can lead to a vicious cycle of stress and feeling overwhelmed.

SUPPORT SYSTEMS
A person's experience of developing depression may be impacted by the support systems they have available, such as the family, friends and colleagues around them. It could include how easy it is to speak to a doctor, counsellor, therapist, or how

easy it is for them to access support from public or private systems in their area.

> "A person can experience depression despite having fantastic support around them – it does not make them immune to becoming depressed."

However, it is important to highlight that a person can experience depression despite having fantastic support around them – it does not make them immune to becoming depressed. This can often be hard for those trying to support them to understand.

ABILITY TO ASK FOR HELP

How able the person feels to say they are struggling and reach out for support about their struggles is also an important factor. In childhood, people learn whether they can talk about or express their emotions, whether they can talk about problems, whether it is 'OK to not be OK', whether it feels safe to share how they feel and so on. These early lessons about emotions often become the narrative and the strategy that a person tries to adopt when they are older. If these early lessons teach a person not to talk about emotions, to try to always smile and be OK and not to make a fuss about their own problems, then this makes it more likely that if a person begins to struggle they will find it hard to talk about this, acknowledge it and reach out for help.

OPPRESSED AND MARGINALIZED GROUPS

For some groups there is an ongoing and insidious culture of oppression, dismissal, power differentials, social disadvantages and inequalities. There are challenges due to poverty or race/culture that limits access to life opportunities. These challenges can make it harder to face the day, to feel hopeful, to believe in a good future, leaving someone feeling depleted, disillusioned, powerless and exhausted.

LIVING IN A FAST-PACED SOCIETY

We live in a fast-paced, over-stimulating, over-accessible society. We are constantly tied to our phones, with a pressure to be available 24/7. The ability to be constantly engaged in world affairs, to be able to comment, share opinions, debate with strangers, to witness trolling, abuse, outrage and much more is exhausting. People are working and parenting and socializing and engaging online in a never-ending daily cycle. It is an overwhelming way to live, the impact of which we are still learning about. Being mindful of this on a person's wellbeing and ability to cope is important.

A SHARED UNDERSTANDING

When you are supporting a person with depression, it can be helpful to understand *their* thoughts or perspectives about why they are experiencing depression. Do they think it is due to life experience, trauma, biology, genetics? Understanding their perspective is important as it can influence the support they may be open to. Therapeutic interventions, particularly through developing psychological formulations, can help a person explore this question of 'why' in more detail.

Ultimately, reaching a shared understanding for the causes of or reasons for depression is just one aspect of the work. A large part of supporting a person is through developing ways to help someone once depression takes its grip. We will talk about this more in Part 2.

Depression is quiet.

Depression is dark.

Depression is painful.

Depression is a whirling storm, a dark cloud, a heavy cloak, a never-ending aching fatigue.

Depression is all-consuming, overwhelming, and yet also numbing, silent, lying creeping beneath the surface, unseen by many.

Depression can filter into every thought, every feeling, every ache in the body.

Depression can hide, slipping behind a smile, a bright performance, behind the constant activity, the rushing around, the achieving.

Depression can tiptoe mildly into a person's life, hints of grey creeping around the edges of a person's thoughts, feelings, activities, relationships, days.

Depression can also grow and thunder in with a terrible bleakness and hopelessness that consumes not only the person with depression but also reaches its darkness toward those around them, causing worry, stress, anxiety, frustration, anger, conflict, withdrawal, despair and heartache.

CHAPTER 3

WHAT IS IT REALLY LIKE TO EXPERIENCE DEPRESSION?

What does depression really look and feel like? What is it like to live with a mind gripped by depression? What might we see in our loved ones, friends and colleagues who have depression? What might we be surprised to see? This chapter will help you answer these questions and more.

SHARING STORIES

To help you understand depression in this intimate way, throughout this chapter I will be introducing you to some incredible people who have bravely agreed to share their stories. Please note, some of the personal and identifying details have been changed to help maintain privacy for each person and their families.

BELLA'S STORY

Bella, aged 33, grew up in the countryside, in a large family. Her parents worked long hours but she had lots of hobbies and attended clubs – she was always busy.

She became a university lecturer and got married. She and her husband began trying for children, but whilst others seemed to get pregnant fairly quickly, it didn't happen for Bella and her husband, and as time passed, and investigations were unable to find a reason for this infertility, Bella found her mood and mental health becoming affected and depression began to grow.

Bella initially sought help for her mental health via her family doctor at the start of her fertility journey, but found the response underwhelming. However, as the depression grew she sought a private counsellor instead who she saw for nearly a year.

"I suffered from depression a few years ago, alongside a diagnosis of unexplained infertility. I don't really remember it starting, but overtime I felt numb and stuck. Things would carry on around me, but I felt at a complete standstill. In order to function, my husband would come with me every morning in the car so I wouldn't be alone with my thoughts during the drive. I found I could cope at work but would shift completely the moment I got back in the car."

THE HEAVY BURDEN OF DEPRESSION

Living with depression is a heavy burden. Take a moment to consider the depression symptoms outlined in Chapter 1 (the feelings, thoughts, physical symptoms and behaviours) that a person with depression may be carrying with them *every single day*. As we know, each of these symptoms can exist on a spectrum from mild to severe and are often invisible. To help understand what this experience might be like, take a moment to reflect on how it may feel *to carry this invisible burden with you each and every day.*

ISHANA'S STORY

Ishana, aged 39, grew up in a busy, loving family. She always had social anxieties and insecurities about herself and her worth, but she managed these well and enjoyed a happy family and social life.

Ishana worked hard and trained to become a therapist for people with mental health difficulties. She became successful at her work and she got married and had three children.

A few years ago, Ishana experienced a number of stressors at the same time – health-related stress, her marriage broke down, she experienced a challenging period at work with a bullying boss and she struggled with support issues within her social group. These issues had an accumulative effect, alongside parenting and working full-time, and Ishana began to experience symptoms of depression (not sleeping, being very tearful, negative thoughts, anxiety).

Over time, Ishana was supported by her friends and colleagues to recognize she was experiencing depression. She began to make changes to look after herself and sought out therapy.

"Depression was invisible. It didn't feel like depression. It was just a bad day. A bad week. Except it was a lot of them. I kept thinking it was just a reaction to stress. It was sitting on the floor having a panic attack while trying to make Sunday lunch. It was immense loneliness despite having lots of friends. It was crying in the car park on the way to get the shopping, feeling unable to function. It was knowing I couldn't stop because I had to keep going. If I didn't keep going, how would I pay the bills, parent, get chores done? It was trying to decide how to reach out and say I'm struggling and yet being silent. It was being snappy, irritable, feeling intense physical bodily stress. It was a tightness in the chest. A pressure in the head. It was being unable to wake up without feeling exhausted. It was insomnia. Night-time waking. Anxiety and nightmares. It was going through the motions and still saying 'I'm fine'."

THE EXPERIENCE OF DEPRESSION

To understand more about the experience of depression, we can look at each of the main symptoms of depression in turn:

- Emotional
- Cognitive
- Physical
- Behavioural

THE EMOTIONAL EXPERIENCE

Depression does not involve just one 'feeling'. It is not just sadness. Depression involves many emotions, including fear, worry, shame, guilt, grief, panic, irritability, anxiety and anger. Depression can make emotions feel overwhelming, intense, unbearable. Feelings of hopelessness are common. Sometimes the different emotions can lead people to fail to realize that what they're experiencing is depression – if anger, irritability or anxiety are more visible, this may mask the unhappiness underneath.

People with depression may also experience the absence of happiness/pleasure, or even the absence of emotion, reporting instead feeling numb, feeling flat or not feeling anything. This can be extremely upsetting in itself: to not feel anything, to not be able to feel enjoyment where they previously would. This can push a person to withdraw even more.

Loneliness is frequently reported. People with depression may feel incredibly lonely, even if they are surrounded by people and appear to be a sociable person. Indeed, sometimes being around people exacerbates the loneliness. Sometimes it emphasizes how they feel different, detached, misunderstood. Or sometimes they can feel momentarily OK in a social situation, but the loneliness after a social event thunders in even more crushingly.

People can experience both the numbness of any emotions and, at another time, the intensity of emotions. Waves of depression-related emotions ebb and flow at any time.

"It is important to keep in mind that just because a person is smiling, it does not mean that they are not struggling."

People with depression may also, at times, be able to smile, laugh, engage in fun activities, tell silly stories, perform as if they are fine, and even find enjoyment in the day (particularly people at the milder end of the depression spectrum). The contrast can come when these brighter moments end, and the depression crashes back in, heavy and draining.

It is important to keep in mind that just because a person is smiling, it does not mean that they are not struggling. They may be laughing, but this does not mean they are not in pain. They may appear more angry or irritable than 'depressed', but this does not mean it is not depression. They may appear to have a 'good day', but this does not mean the depression has gone.

GERALDINE'S STORY

Geraldine, aged 75, has a big family of children and grandchildren. All her life it has been important to her to be busy, to be looking after people, to be useful. She had a successful career as a nurse.

The year after Geraldine retired, she experienced a rare illness that caused her significant physical impairments, making looking after herself or caring for others really difficult. She had to learn to rely on carers and on her family supporting her, rather than the other way round. This was really upsetting for Geraldine.

Geraldine kept herself busy, she kept smiling and doing all the things people expected of her, but at times she would become overwhelmed and very tearful. Her family became concerned and supported her to see a counsellor who identified that she was experiencing depression, despite how she positively presented to the world.

"I'm good at keeping going, smiling. I want to look after the people I care about. I want to do so much. But I know I can't do it how I want to and it's so frustrating. I get so cross with myself. I find it hard to explain to people close to me how devastated and sad I feel. They don't always see it. But sometimes I just don't want to carry on. I'm holding everyone back. I think it would be better if I weren't here, although I know everyone tells me they want me here. I feel so useless, and I end up constantly thinking about what I can't do. It's just so hard."

THE COGNITIVE EXPERIENCE

Cognitive symptoms of depression include thoughts, beliefs, perceptions, memories and thinking processes. It is all the things that go through, invade, take over, a person's mind throughout the day and night. Typically, in depression, the internal thoughts and narrative will be heavily biased toward the negative, often with core negative beliefs through which everything becomes filtered. Thoughts related to not being good enough, a failure, a bad person and being useless are common underlying core beliefs. You may hear it in the way a person speaks: 'I can't get anything right', 'I'm so useless', 'I'm such a failure/loser/idiot'. Negative thoughts can be about how the person sees themselves and how they view others; they often make unfavourable comparisons to themselves. They may view the world as an unsafe, scary place.

If you imagine all your thoughts are filtered through a negative, dark, bleak filter – a filter that will draw terrible conclusions or perceive things in the worst, most catastrophic way about you, others, the world around you, the future, the past – then you will be some way toward understanding what the mind can be like in depression. A person isn't consciously filtering thoughts in this way; the depressed mind is automatically doing this for them. And it's really, really tough. To live with this internal critical, bleak, bullying monologue can be overwhelming, difficult and distressing. These negative internal narratives can lead to low self-esteem, lack of self-confidence, anxiety, paranoia, and high levels of self-doubt. Thoughts about worthlessness and hopelessness are frequently experienced. And some of the most difficult types of thoughts that arise in depression are about self-harming and suicidal ideation (see Chapter 4).

Depression can also impact on thinking processes in other ways – attention and concentration are often affected, speed of processing information is slowed down, and often people describe feeling as if they are in a fog, like their brain is working slowly. People report concerns with their memory, including difficulties learning new information, remembering tasks they need to do, conversations they have had, what they have been doing or need to do. Decision-making and problem-solving feel more difficult. Organization becomes problematic due to all these factors and as a result a person can feel disorganized, overly stressed, unable to cope, unable to complete or stay on top of tasks. Often people worry that these cognitive difficulties are a sign there is something wrong with the brain (for example, a worry that they are developing dementia is a very common fear, even in younger people who are depressed). However, these cognitive changes are rarely due to permanent brain changes. They are frequently due to the impact of the depression itself. Importantly, once the depression has lifted, these thinking processes will return to their typical level of functioning.

Jamie Day, mental health advocate, writer and podcaster, told me:

> "I've had depression my entire adult life (even if at the time I didn't know it), which has meant varying ups and downs, but my most severe lows have been because of difficult relationships and bullying at work. When depression descends a range of emotions swell in my head and I find it difficult to find any clarity amongst the noise. When that feeling lingers, a sadness takes over and both mentally and physically I feel unable to function."
>
> Jamie Day

THE PHYSICAL EXPERIENCE

Physical – or somatic – symptoms of depression are often the most misunderstood. We are learning all the time about the links between body and mind, and we know that when the mind is struggling, we can feel this in the body. Physical symptoms can include:

- The body feeling tired, heavy and lethargic
- Aches, pains and tension
- Moving more slowly or being very physically restless, constantly moving
- Headaches and stomach problems
- Changes in appetite, leading to weight loss, or cravings to overeat, especially sugary high-calorie foods leading to weight gain
- Loss of sexual function/drive/libido
- Changes in sleep patterns, with difficulties falling asleep at the beginning of the night, waking in the night, or early-morning wakening
- Low energy and motivation, along with exhaustion or fatigue, even after sleeping well

"It is important to keep in mind that for a person with depression every action may be a struggle physically."

45

Some people may experience predominantly physical symptoms, with less awareness of the cognitive or emotional symptoms. For others, the physical symptoms may be minimal.

It is important to keep in mind that for a person with depression every action may be a struggle physically. The effort of getting up, getting dressed, having a shower, getting through the day when the body aches, everything feels slowed down, sleep has become non-existent, appetite has disappeared, they constantly feel hollow or sick – all of these physical symptoms make the day a little harder. Yet these are all invisible symptoms. You may not know a person is feeling this way. They may not even be able to acknowledge or put it into words, or connect the physical with the emotional. They may think they are physically sick or seek help for the physical symptoms without acknowledging the depression present.

KAAMIL'S STORY

Kaamil, aged 35, grew up in a small town and has happy memories of his close-knit family and friends, although he remembers being anxious and shy, at times, and not feeling confident. He moved to a big city in his 20s and although he was pretty successful in his work as a musician, and enjoyed it, other areas of his life were coming undone – he was unhappy in his relationship, his living situation and his friendships.

In his 30s, depression grew. Kaamil tried to ignore or dismiss it and convince himself he was OK. It grew bigger. Eventually it overwhelmed him. Kaamil sought help, through therapy first, and later therapy alongside medication, and he slowly began to find a way through the depression. He found he was able to make positive changes to areas of his life that were causing him difficulty and he was able to learn strategies to help himself. Life became brighter again.

"Depression came into my life slowly, over a period of a few years. Looking back now, I can see how it came in, as the stress built, issues arose with where I lived, relationships, feeling unsupported, feeling trapped, powerless, unhappy with choices being made… I was trying to carry on, trying to convince myself everything was OK but eventually my mind and body said 'enough'. I crashed hard, struggling to get up – I just couldn't function, it was terrifying. Anxiety and panic kept gripping me. Leaving my flat became impossible. Some days I would be curled up on the floor unable to move. My mind was noisy, constantly whirling.

The mornings were worst. I would wake up early and for a second there would be a moment when I wondered if I was OK, and then it was like a computer uploading. I could feel the feelings, the thoughts consuming me, building up inside, becoming so overwhelming. I could feel it in my chest, my head, the pit of my stomach, in my jaw. I struggled to think straight. I questioned everything. I worried about everything. I didn't feel like I could trust my own mind."

THE BEHAVIOURAL EXPERIENCE

The behavioural symptoms of depression are often misunderstood or perceived negatively. They may include:

- Withdrawing and feeling unable to be around people, leading to avoiding situations, cancelling plans, missing events, unanswered text messages and calls, and not answering the door to people
- Withdrawing from/not taking part in usual hobbies or previously enjoyed activities
- Getting behind on, or not achieving tasks at home or work or school; taking longer to complete tasks, avoiding tasks or working longer hours to try to keep up
- Being late for work/school and/or frequent sick days
- Being very quiet and not 'joining in' when in social situations
- Loss of temper
- Drinking too much or taking drugs
- A lack of self-care, such as not washing, staying in bed during the day or not cleaning/tidying up for prolonged periods
- For some, impulsive or risky behaviours (e.g. drinking frequently, engaging in one night stands), due to wanting to feel numb or not caring about themselves or their self-worth because of the depression

When these behaviours happen, it can feel like the person with depression is avoiding you, withdrawing, letting you down and being unreliable. It can feel frustrating to see the self-destructive behaviours, or the inability to look after themselves. You may feel disappointed, let down, pushed away and unwanted.

"When the person with depression behaves in these ways, they are just doing the best they can to keep going, to survive, to get to the end of the day."

However, we can understand these behaviours as responses to the emotional, physical and cognitive symptoms of depression:

- They often mask the unhappiness, sadness and numbness underneath.
- They may act to shield the person from the negative thoughts – a way of feeling something, feeling wanted, or of protecting themselves from the fears, comparisons and critical voice the depression feeds into their mind.
- They may be a way to respond to the physical symptoms of the depression.

- Substance use can provide temporary relief from difficult thoughts and feelings, but this is often short-lived and feeds back into the depression cycle.

Ultimately, we know that these behavioural responses are not going to be effective in the longer term, in coping with the symptoms of depression. However, it is key to understand that when the person with depression behaves in these ways, they are just doing the best they can to keep going, to survive, to get to the end of the day.

BEN'S STORY

Ben, aged 42, moved around a lot as a child and never felt like he settled or fitted in. He didn't feel very supported at home.

Ben worked hard and became a medical professional. He struggled with low mood and anxiety during his training, but did well with some counselling.

Just before the 2020 Covid-19 pandemic, Ben experienced a number of difficult experiences all at once. He was given more responsibilities at work, which he wanted but turned out to be very stressful and high pressured. He also experienced some unexpected health issues, which were worrying and meant he had to make some adaptions to his working practices.

The stress built up, alongside the stress of the pandemic, and slowly he noticed he was becoming more and more anxious and low in mood. He began to doubt his abilities, struggled to focus at work and eventually the family doctor diagnosed depression.

"When I think about my depression, I think about the blankness. There are things I want to say or write, but nothing comes out. I can sit and get lost in my mind for hours. I want to connect with my friends, I want to feel connected with my partner, but there is nothing, and this makes me feel terrible, and guilty and sad. I try to do things, but can't find my motivation. Small tasks become overwhelming, so I avoid, avoid, avoid. When I do something, I go through the motions but I can't find enjoyment. I can't sleep as my mind is racing and I'm so agitated. It's utterly terrible."

MASKING DEPRESSION

One of the challenges you may face in understanding and supporting someone with depression is when the person doesn't *look* depressed. They might smile, laugh, socialize, get up for work every day. They might appear busy, they might take on more tasks, they might achieve, or tell you they're fine. They appear to have a great night out, a great weekend – they post smiley pictures on social media. They exercise, they parent, they do DIY, they work. They care for others, ask questions, listen, worry about others, provide support. They leave you thinking, 'Well they can't be depressed!'

But wait. This is what depression can look like too. Often the milder end of depression, for sure. But actually, sometimes people can mask an overwhelming depression, for a limited period of time, very well too.

The functioning person with depression can outwardly mask the sadness, worry, fatigue and anxiety. They can hide the tears, put on a smile, go through all the motions. They can have good moments, hours, days, a good weekend. Having moments of laughter, joy and lightness, however, does not mean there is not sadness, heaviness, bleakness and grey. It does not mean there is not fear, panic, tearfulness, shame and guilt. It does not mean sleep is their friend, that movement is not hard, decisions do not torment, and tiredness is not overwhelming. The functioning person with depression may keep going, for now, but this does not make their depression any less real. It does sometimes make it harder to understand – even for the person themselves. Harder for people around them to grasp. Harder for people to empathize with and hold compassion for. The functioning person with depression may fear letting you see exactly how they feel, and try to protect you from this. They may have days when they crash, withdraw, become tearful or panicked, agitated, angry, irritable or sad. They may struggle, and hide and sleep – and then they may put on the smile and off they go. Functioning again.

> "The functioning person with depression may keep going, for now, but this does not make their depression any less real."

'BUT I'M NOT DEPRESSED'

A person may be depressed and not fully know it. It is possible for them to not feel 'bad enough' to be depressed; to feel they don't have enough 'reason' to be depressed. They may feel they don't have the 'time' to be depressed or that they can't be depressed because they don't have *all* the symptoms people associate with depression. It is possible not to remember what life felt like when depression wasn't there and so feeling like this is just life. They may not know they are depressed because they are functioning. They many think that 'Depression happens to other people'. It is possible to know what depression is in others and not recognize it within themselves.

ROSIE'S STORY

Rosie, aged 21, grew up in a nice house with lots of 'nice things'. However, she felt lonely at home, never quite good enough and didn't feel like she experienced positive attention or love.

Rosie experienced trauma in her teens and became rebellious as a teenager, often fighting with her parents. She had a series of relationships in which she wasn't treated well. She often felt like she had no value or worth. She expected men to disappoint her and treat her badly.

After a particularly upsetting relationship break-up, amidst work and health stresses, Rosie found her mood deteriorated. She saw a private psychiatrist and was diagnosed with depression.

Rosie lost her appetite as a result of the depression and barely ate or moved or looked after herself. She agreed to a short admission to a private mental health facility and then continued with therapy and medication once she was discharged. Slowly she began to believe in herself again.

CHAPTER 4

UNDERSTANDING RISK OF HARM TO SELF IN DEPRESSION

The most significant risk of harm that affects a person with depression, and of course causes significant worry for anyone supporting them, is the risk of self-harm or suicide. My aim is to help you make sense of these difficulties, to manage them and give you ideas of how you can help and find support, whether you are dealing with this now or in the future. It is also really important to look after yourself.

Caution: Always seek specific professional advice from a qualified medical or health professional if you believe the person you are supporting is at risk of self-harm or suicide.

Please note: This chapter contains references to methods of self-harm and suicide.

At times when the darkness closes in
The depression may fill your mind with dark, heavy
thoughts.
'You can escape this',
The depression whispers.
'It will be better for everyone'.
'You don't deserve to be here'. It persuades
and shouts and draws you deeper along
the dark road.

It is important to make a distinction between self-harm and suicide. People with depression can experience self-harm thoughts and behaviours, and they can experience suicidal ideation and behaviours. However not everyone who experiences depression experiences self-harm; people who self-harm don't necessarily have suicidal intentions; and not everyone who experiences depression considers suicide.

SELF-HARM

Self-harm refers to any behaviours that cause harm to the individual, typically *without* the intention of suicide. Behaviours include, for example, cutting, scratching and burning, which are the focus of this section, but a person may also self-harm through the use of alcohol, drugs, self-neglect, bingeing or undereating as a form of self-punishment.

A person may engage in self-harm behaviours for different reasons, including:

- To numb their feelings/stop the pain
- To cope with overwhelming feelings, thoughts or memories
- To feel something
- To punish themselves (e.g. when the depression tells them how terrible they are)

Self-harm may be triggered by something that happens, something someone says or does, or it could be triggered by internal thoughts or memories. The person may then experience a range of distressing thoughts and emotions, including thoughts or urges to self-harm.

Self-harm can be very difficult to talk about or disclose. People who self-harm may be very ashamed of their behaviours and will go to great lengths to hide this. They may be worried about their behaviour being misunderstood or upsetting those close to them, so may not talk about it. Some do find they can talk about and disclose self-harm more easily.

Unfortunately, self-harm can provoke difficult or complex reactions in the support systems around a person, including the professional community. At its worst, it can cause people to lose empathy and compassion and can lead to punishing responses. People sometimes refer to self-harm behaviour as a way of gaining attention. It is not this. As noted above, people often, in fact, keep their self-harm very private. Language such as 'attention seeking' is unhelpful and stigmatizing and causes people around the person to be unable to fully empathize with the pain and suffering they are going through and therefore not provide effective support. It is important to remember that often there are many reasons for self-harm as noted previously; however, even if the self-harm is also a way of showing their pain to others, this is a message we need to listen to, pay attention to, and respond to with care and compassion.

HOW TO HELP

If the person you are caring for is engaging in self-harming behaviours, you may find the following ideas helpful:

- Firstly, please know you are not expected to know all the answers/solutions. Therapeutic support for understanding and managing self-harm is a skilled, trained approach and you are not expected to be an expert.
- If you can, let the person talk about what is happening, what they have been doing, even though it might be upsetting. Try to listen without judgement.
- Be aware this may be very difficult for the person with depression to talk about, and it may be very difficult for you to listen to. Looking after yourself is important.

- Whilst self-harm can cause physical harm, be painful or disfiguring, it is typically not designed to end the person's life. If you think it might be, see the advice on suicidal behaviours on page 60.
- With their permission for you to help, you could problem-solve some next steps. These might include:
  ○ Reading up about self-harm together, using reputable mental health resources.
  ○ Thinking about something the person could try to do instead when they feel an urge to self-harm (see box overleaf).
  ○ Finding numbers for crisis or text lines that they could use if they have the urge to self-harm (see Resources).
  ○ Helping them seek professional support (see Chapter 11).
- It may help to read and learn more about self-harm yourself.
- Look after yourself and reach out for your own support as needed. Remember, again, that you are not expected to have all the solutions or ability to stop these behaviours.

"Whilst self-harm can cause physical harm, be painful or disfiguring, it is typically not designed to end the person's life."

TACKLING THE URGE TO SELF-HARM

When someone feels like self-harming, they could try one of the following actions instead:

- Choose to remove access to possible equipment that may be used in self-harm.
- Hold ice cubes (this is an unpleasant but not damaging action).
- Take a cold shower/splash the face with very cold water.
- Do an intense short burst of exercise (e.g. ten star jumps, fast run on the spot).
- Draw on the arm or part of the body instead of harming it.
- Practise breathing/grounding exercises while using a calming scent.
- Write down thoughts, feelings and urges.
- Agree to sit with someone and engage in another activity/talk until the urge to harm has passed.
- Contact a crisis line.

SUICIDAL THOUGHTS AND BEHAVIOURS

It is extremely distressing and overwhelming to hear a person you care about talk about wanting to end their life. You may feel sadness, fear, anxiety, panic, dread, anger, frustration, and more. There may be a sense of disbelief that the person is even experiencing these feelings or considering these thoughts. Although there are things you can look out for and ways you can help, remember you are not expected to have all the answers or to be able to stop these experiences. There are skilled professionals who can and should provide this support and it is important to liaise with them as needed.

WHAT IS SUICIDE RISK?

There are four key aspects to consider when understanding suicidal thoughts and behaviours, which will help you have an idea of how risky a situation is:

1. Is the person having suicidal thoughts/images (known as suicidal ideation)?
2. Has the person thought about ways to end their life (the method, plans, how they would do this)?
3. Has the person got the *means* to carry out their plans? (Do they have access to a way to do this, such medication, or equipment?)
4. Does the person *want* to act on these thoughts/plans (intent)? If so, is this now or have they made a timescale for this?

Ultimately, the more of these factors that are present, the more risk there is. For example, a person can experience suicidal ideation (e.g. thoughts about suicide, fleeting thoughts or images, considering not being here any longer, wanting the pain to stop) without a plan/method/means of what they would do and without having any intent to act on these thoughts. If anything, they will have clear reasons why they would *never* act on these thoughts (e.g. because they understand the depression can get better, because they would never leave loved ones, because they don't want to act on them).

Some people with depression, however, may have suicidal thoughts and then go on to *plan* how to end their life and have the *intent and the means to act* on these plans. This is, of course, very worrying and the risk is much higher when a person has this level of suicidal plans and intent. Generally (although not always) as the depression becomes more severe, so may the level of suicidal risk increase.

WHY ARE THEY THINKING ABOUT SUICIDE?

Often understanding *why* the person is thinking about suicide can be bewildering, especially when from the outside it appears that they have so much going for them.

It is important to understand that suicidal thoughts are part of what depression brings. Depression is sending these thoughts to the mind. If the depression wasn't present, the person wouldn't be experiencing or listening to these thoughts in the same way. Note that it is possible for the mind to send suicidal thoughts when a person is not depressed, but the person will tend to pay very little attention to the thought, dismiss it and carry on with their day.

When depression sends suicidal thoughts, it is the depressed mind trying to think of a way to solve the problem of depression. Depression affects cognition (see page 6) and can lead to faulty or rigid thinking and poor problem-solving, which makes it hard for the person with depression to consider any other way out, or for them to imagine things getting better. At times the thoughts about suicide can be overwhelming and intrusive.

> "When depression sends suicidal thoughts, it is the depressed mind trying to think of a way to solve the problem of depression."

Depression can make a person feel hopeless about themselves or their future, or it can make the future feel unbearable (especially if there is a fear of future problems or losses, for example future physical ill-health/pain or requiring others to care for them and not wanting to be a burden; being arrested, losing a job or financial losses, or loss of status; online bullying or shaming leading to a loss of how they or others may perceive them).

It can also be about wanting the pain of depression to stop, and seeing no other way to achieve this than to die. At other times the depression will convince the person that this is the best or only solution to the difficulties they are facing and/or that their loved ones will be better off without them. They may understand that their suicide may cause pain to others, but the depression convinces them that this will not last and their loved ones will be able to move on and recover. The person may even say this to you, which can be very painful to hear. We know that this statement is not true for people who are bereaved by suicide, but we need to try to understand that in those moments, depression can be a persuasive voice.

HOW TO HELP

If the person you are helping expresses any element of suicidal ideation, it is important (and I know this is hard) to try to stay calm.

- Take a breath, ground yourself, give yourself a moment.
- Believe them. You don't have to understand, you don't have to make sense of it, you don't have to feel comfortable – you can feel all sorts of emotions, but whatever you do, believe them.

- Acknowledge how hard this must be for them. Let
  them talk to you. Ask what they are experiencing and
  find out what the depression is telling them. Empathize
  with compassion. Let them know you are so sad they
  are going through this.

KNOW THAT IT IS OK TO ASK QUESTIONS

Do not be afraid to ask questions to help you understand the
situation. I know this will be upsetting, but the more you can
understand, the more you can support the best course of action.

However, if you do not feel you can have a conversation about
this, or it does not feel appropriate in your role (e.g. you may be
a colleague who is unsure how far to explore this) please don't
worry – go straight to seeking help, as outlined below.

Remember: Even if you feel able to ask questions, it is important
that you do not take on the pressure or responsibility to solve this
or make it better. That is not and cannot be your role. You are just
trying to help and be supportive; you are just asking questions to
understand more. *You will still need to seek professional help and
the ideas below are not a substitute for that.*

If you do feel able, you can ask something like:

- 'I'm worried about you and I know depression can
  send some pretty scary thoughts. I want to help and
  understand. I'm here for you, can we talk about this?'

- 'Are you having thoughts about not wanting to be here anymore/wanting to die?'
- 'Have you had these thoughts before?'
- 'Are there times when these thoughts are worse/stronger? (e.g. at night, after drinking alcohol, when alone?)'
- 'Do you feel safe or do you feel scared about these thoughts making you do something terrible?'
- 'Are you thinking about ways you could make this happen? Ways of ending your life? If so, what are these?'
- 'Do you want to act on these thoughts or are you worried you might?'
- 'Do you want to act on these thoughts now? Or in the future?' (This helps you understand whether the risk is immediate.)
- 'Have you started doing anything to make this happen?' (e.g. bought medication)
- 'Is there anything that would stop you acting on these thoughts?'

You can ask any of these, or variation of these in any order as needed.

Asking these questions will help you and the person with depression understand more about what is going on in their mind and whether urgent support is needed. Try to ask questions with empathy, compassion, kindness, and without judgement, as this will enable the person to be the most honest with you.

Remember: Suicidal thoughts may well be in the person's mind whether you ask about them or not, so do not be afraid to ask.

TALK TO OTHERS

Don't be afraid to talk to other close family or friends, to find out about their experience of suicidal thoughts with the person. If you are worried and have an idea, or know that the person is experiencing suicidal ideation it can help to talk to others close to them. Ask if the person has voiced or attempted suicide before or spoken about this with others. Involving others helps to increase the support around a person and ensures that everyone can be alert to risk. Of course, this does not mean telling everyone a person is feeling suicidal. But you can talk to those people who you know play a key supportive role.

> "Remember you do not have to carry this burden alone and cannot promise to do so. You can support them to seek help or you can do this on their behalf."

Most importantly, remember you do not have to carry this burden alone and cannot promise to do so. Sometimes a person will start sharing their thoughts and may ask you to keep them to yourself. You might agree, not knowing what they are going to tell you, and then feel stuck to know how to help without breaking their trust. It is difficult, but it is important to gently let them know you cannot keep this to yourself. You can support them to seek help or you can do this on their behalf.

TAKING ACTION

If it is clear that a person is experiencing suicidal thoughts, it is important to seek professional help and support or support them to access help. The urgency of seeking help may depend on the severity of the thoughts.

If the person has made plans and/or has an intent to act on the thoughts (particularly if their plans are possible/feasible), or they tell you that they do not feel they can keep themselves safe, *seek urgent crisis support.*

If possible, you can also talk about making a plan for what to do if the thoughts or urges to act get stronger. You can talk together about who they can or will contact if this happens and how they will keep safe.

You can access help via:

- A medical practitioner (e.g. GP/family doctor).
- Calling emergency services or by going to hospital (Emergency Departments should have a trained clinician available).
- Accessing a therapist/psychologist who offers crisis support.

- Calling or texting a charity helpline or mental health crisis line (see Resources). There are also often mental health crisis lines provided by local mental health services.

Where there is a risk of harm to life, you can make contact with health professionals on the person's behalf, *even if they do not consent*. Confidentiality does not have to be maintained if there is a risk to life. The health professional will be able to advise you from there.

FEAR OF DISCLOSURE

It is common for people to be fearful of disclosing suicidal thoughts (or even disclosing the depression itself) for fear of judgement or consequence (e.g. on their ability to parent, or on their ability to do their job). It is very important to reassure them that:

1. Medical and health professionals understand that depression (and suicidal ideation) is a common experience.
2. Whilst of course it is very sad and something to take seriously, a medical or health professional will not be surprised by a disclosure of suicidal ideation when depression is present. They know that it can be part

---

of depression, and that talking about it and seeking support helps to overcome the risks, so disclosure is a positive sign.

3. Disclosure of these thoughts does not mean the person is not a good parent or is not able to work. It means they are struggling and need help and support.

4. Workplace legislation for mental health is aimed at supporting and protecting people. Adaptations and time off can be arranged if a person is struggling severely.

REPEATED CONVERSATIONS AND COMPLACENCY

You may have conversations about risk with the person you are supporting several times during the depression journey. This can lead to two main challenges:

1. The impact on your own mental health – feeling worn down, overwhelmed and devastated by the ongoing or repeated suicidal thoughts.

2. It may lead to complacency – a sense that this is talked about so much, but is never going to happen. It is possible to begin to stop really listening or taking it seriously, which of course can lead to increased risk as it might be possible to miss the signs when things get worse.

Most importantly, if you are feeling worn down in any of these ways, it is important to ensure that you access help and support and that you encourage the person with depression to seek help and support. Make sure the risk keeps being communicated to professionals who are trained to assess and manage it. As I have already highlighted, you cannot and should not carry this alone. And you need to look after yourself.

PART 2

HOW YOU CAN HELP

CHAPTER 5

YOUR ROLE AS A SUPPORTER

When you support a person with depression, you bring yourself to the situation. You will have your own thoughts, feelings, reactions, views and perspectives (e.g. about depression, mental health and how to support someone) that you bring to the experience. To understand this fully, it can be helpful to reflect on the following:

- What you bring to the situation
  - Your understanding of mental health and depression
  - How mental health, depression and coping has been talked about and understood growing up
  - How you would like to be supported in the same situation
  - How supporting someone with depression affects you

- o Your skills and strengths
- o Your life journey
- The support journey
- Your responsibilities and boundaries

The more we understand about ourselves, what we bring and offer in our helping role, and what impacts on our ability to do this, the more we can develop and enhance our skills as a supporter. This helps us do our best to help our loved ones.

WHAT YOU BRING

YOUR UNDERSTANDING OF MENTAL HEALTH AND DEPRESSION

It is helpful to understand that your knowledge of depression and mental health may shape how you feel about it, and how you may offer support. If this knowledge is limited or fixed in some way, or if we (deep down) hold stereotypes, judgements or stigmatized views of mental health or depression, it is going to have a negative impact on the ability to support others. Reflecting on this, and developing your knowledge and understanding of mental health or depression from informed sources, can be very important for you in your helping role.

WHAT YOU LEARNT ABOUT MENTAL HEALTH, DEPRESSION AND COPING STRATEGIES GROWING UP

We are all influenced by our childhood experiences. How mental health and/or depression was talked about growing up will have an impact. How you were taught to cope, to deal with challenges or stress, to show or talk about emotion, or to talk about problems will all have an impact on how you may offer support. As with all childhood experiences and learning, we may repeat this into adulthood or we may take a completely different stance, or some middle ground between the two. Taking time to reflect on this can be helpful to understand how your early life experiences may influence your perspectives and how you may view mental health, depression or coping strategies in others because of this.

HOW YOU WOULD LIKE TO BE SUPPORTED IN THE SAME SITUATION

"Keep in mind that we are all individual in what we may want, need and find helpful, and what works for us may not work for someone else."

How we offer support can be influenced by what we think we would want or need in the same situation. How you would want to be communicated with, how you would want to talk about your difficulties or emotions, how you would want others to help or keep their distance, what you would need for yourself, and also what you think you would not find helpful, or would not like. This can impact the support you may instinctively offer or how you respond to someone who is struggling. This can include what external support you believe is helpful or unhelpful (e.g. therapy, exercise, medication).

Keep in mind that we are all individual in what we may want, need and find helpful, and what works for us may not work for someone else. What you would find most helpful may not work for the person you are supporting. They may need you to take a different approach.

"I found it helpful to talk to my friends about how I was doing, and because of circumstances this was often via text. I was often alone without adult company so being asked how I was and taking the time to talk/text was really important for me. However, I know that some of the people in my support group didn't like to talk on text or they didn't like to talk when they were struggling and so thought I would be the same. I found their approach difficult and they found what I needed out of their comfort zone. This made me feel more isolated at times."
Ishana

HOW BEING AROUND SOMEONE WITH DEPRESSION AFFECTS YOU

We know that helping someone with depression is tough. It can be stressful, worrying, upsetting and overwhelming. Worrying about the impact of the depression, seeing how it weighs so heavily can be heartbreaking, terrifying and exhausting. You may feel like you are walking on eggshells, scared of saying or doing the wrong thing or of making things worse. You may be seeing messages not returned, plans cancelled at the last minute, meetings missed, work days taken off sick, social occasions missed, advice not taken, food provided not eaten. You may hear the same negative thoughts or see the same distress again and again, despite all the reassurance or support or encouragement you give.

"You may feel like you are walking on eggshells, scared of saying or doing the wrong thing or of making things worse."

Depression can also make a person self-focused, which can be hurtful. And there is no doubt this can all take its toll. You may feel filled with empathy and love, and you may also feel frustrated, saddened, irritated, disappointed, disheartened and despairing. It can make you feel helpless, rejected, annoyed and powerless. You will likely also have your own thoughts and feelings about the depression and its behaviours, and about the person with depression, which might feel disloyal or critical. You may have lots of negative thoughts such as: 'Maybe they aren't trying enough' or 'They don't care about me' or 'They are so selfish'. It might make you think they are never going to get better, that it is hopeless – and then these thoughts bring sadness or anger, guilt and shame. You may experience the physical stress and tension in your body, the tiredness, the sleeplessness. And all this may lead you to step up your support, or it can make you take a step back, to withdraw, to feel unable to give any more.

"I know I am really disconnected and I struggle with that because I can see how much it upsets my partner. I feel really narcissistic, so inward looking, and I hate it; it's not me, but I'm struggling to shake it off."
Ben

"Seeing the depression every day, watching it take more and more of the partner I know is heartbreaking. I get angry, sad, frustrated. I try to hold on to hope that he will get back to the person I knew. Then when things get difficult, and the depression seems to get worse, I lose hope that he will return to the person he was."
Phoebe, Ben's partner

This is the impact of depression beyond the impact on the person themselves. It is important to be kind and honest with yourself, to acknowledge this and be aware of it. Once you understand this, you can notice when it impacts the support you are able to offer, or when it is becoming overwhelming for you. That way you can ensure that both you and the person you are helping get the support you need.

> *"Supporting a family member is intensely painful at times. For me, being a supporter, it's almost too painful to watch. Over many years I've supported my family member, either living in my home or remotely. I remember making countless cups of tea in an attempt to find something to do, something to tempt them to sit up in bed. I've held them when they didn't have the energy to hold their own body up. I've listened to them tell me that there is such darkness that they can see no purpose for anything. I would often go away and cry and then I would pull myself together and carry on. When we've reflected on those times, I know that helping them feeling safe and loved was a vital part of coming through, even though I felt helpless. There were many times when I wanted to just take hold and say, 'Come on, enough now, let's not do this anymore.' Of course, my timetable for recovery was never theirs. And they did emerge again."*
>
> Suzy, who has supported someone with depression

YOUR SKILLS AND STRENGTHS

You will bring your own skills and strengths to your helping role which you can draw on. You may also find yourself in situations that you don't feel skilled in, which may make you feel uncomfortable or anxious. Being aware of your strengths and where you may feel less skilled or comfortable can be helpful when offering support, to work to your strengths but acknowledge where you may struggle.

This awareness can help you as supporter to identify when you may need to step out of your comfort zone and learn new skills. For example, if you are not comfortable when people express emotion, it may help to acknowledge this is hard for you, and then this could be a skill that you focus on developing, so you can be comfortable with sitting and listening to the person when they need it.

When supporting a person with depression the following skills and strengths may be useful (we will talk more about these in the next chapters):

- Good listener
- Calm in a crisis
- Good communicator
- Encouraging and supportive
- Persistent – not giving up
- Patient
- Kind

- Empathic and compassionate
- Resilient
- Understanding and forgiving
- Good at problem-solving when needed
- Able to tolerate and sit with difficult emotions
- Able to practise self-care and look after yourself

YOUR LIFE JOURNEY

When you are supporting a person with depression you are dedicating your time, care and resources to helping another person. It is an incredible thing to do, but it doesn't exist in a vacuum. Life goes on – and your life, your challenges, your emotions and your needs are important.

Depending on what is happening in your own life, you may have more or less resources to draw on and time to offer. Reflecting on your own needs, as well as what you have to offer, is important.

Remember: Taking time to make sure that *you* are OK and that *your* needs are prioritized is OK. Taking time for yourself or your immediate family or relationships is OK.

THE SUPPORT JOURNEY

When you are supporting a person with depression, you will be sharing their journey. It will not be a smooth road.

The journey may be a long and winding road, where you are travelling together, but on different paths, sometimes side by side, sometimes moving at different paces, navigating forests and hills and fallen trees, and storms, and detours, to reach brighter skies and smoother roads.
Sometimes the road may feel endless.
Sometimes it may be hard to see the end of the road over the horizon.
Sometimes you may feel you are going in circles or stuck on the same stretch of path.
Sometimes there may be mountains to climb.
Sometimes there are brighter skies, but they only stay for a short while, before the road gets dark again.
Until, eventually, you will both make it to the sunshine and can sit side by side in the light, reflecting on the journey you have both taken.

The metaphor of the winding road shows us there are times when the support journey may be easier and times when it may be more challenging. It also shows us it is not just a straight road from depression to recovery. It is not linear. It is rarely this. However, despite all the twists and turns, it is *always moving forward*. Within the journey, a 'backward step' does not mean you are not still moving forward; it just means that the depression journey is not as simple as each day being better than the last. This isn't what recovery looks like.

"Within the journey, a 'backward step' does not mean you are not still moving forward."

Recognizing the reality of the support journey can help us to know what we may be facing. However, it is also important to know that you do not need to be the only one on the journey with the person you are supporting. Other people can be on the journey too.

It is also important to know that you can, ultimately, step off the path and take some time out for you, at any time.

RESPONSIBILITIES AND BOUNDARIES

Understanding the limits of responsibility as a supporter and how to get the balance right by ensuring you have some boundaries in place is an important part of this journey.

RESPONSIBILITY

When you are supporting a person with depression, the weight of responsibility can feel heavy and sometimes it can feel like yours alone. You may notice you are often consumed with worry, with feeling responsible for making sure the person you are helping is OK, putting their needs first, their mental health first, even at the expense of your own.

- You may be a parent and feel the strength of your responsibility to make things better for your child.
- You may be a sibling or a partner who is constantly striving to make things feel OK for your loved one.
- You may be a loyal friend or a committed colleague who aims to provide support and drop everything when needed.

You might feel the weight of responsibility to be supportive and be there 100 per cent of the time. You might feel you must be there to help contain, cope with or rescue a situation because you may worry about what will happen if you don't; or that no one else can help as well as you; or you might fear that doing less would reflect negatively on you.

The drive to feel responsible, to support whenever it is needed, is a wonderful quality. However, at times, it has the potential to be overwhelming. You may miss the fact that other people can and should help. You may end up prioritizing the needs of the person you are helping at a cost to yourself. Yet, as you may know deep down, it is hard to look after anyone else when your own mental health is suffering.

"You cannot pour from an empty cup. Take care of yourself first."

It is really important to know that there are other people/ professionals (doctors, therapists, mental health services) who have a responsibility to help and other places that can provide support. There may be other people (friends and family) in the person's life. And there is a level of responsibility that also lies with the person with depression themselves.

SUZY'S STORY

Suzy supported her loved one with depression for many years, as their mental health fluctuated. She sought her own therapy as the impact took its toll on her. Through therapy she was supported to identify that she was holding a high level of personal responsibility for wanting to solve her loved one's problems and make their distress better. Incredibly empathic, Suzy felt the pain very intensely. However, over time she began to feel overwhelmed and resentful, not feeling able to bear the distress anymore. With support, Suzy was able to recognize that she did not have to hold all the responsibility for supporting her loved one, and that at times of crisis she could share this with mental health services as well. She also was supported to recognize the value of looking after herself, taking a break and stepping back when she needed.

FINDING THE RIGHT BALANCE

Finding a way to determine how much you put into your helping role is a unique and individual balancing act. To do this, you will need to balance:

- What the person may need, how they most benefit from being supported, and the severity of the depression
- How much the person is able to engage in supporting themselves or reaching out to others
- What the person most needs right now
- Your own needs and challenges, your own mental health needs, and your own life journey
- What you can realistically do, whilst looking after yourself
- Who else is in the person's support system including family, partners and friends
- What other professional resources are available, including public and private support, charity support or crisis helplines

Finding the right balance for how much support you can give means weighing up all these factors, and finding what is right for you.

CHAPTER 6

KEY MESSAGES

As we begin to explore ways you can offer support, I want to share some key messages to keep in mind.

NO 'ONE SIZE FITS ALL'

There is no 'one size fits all' way of helping someone with depression. Every person is different and will have a unique way they like to be supported. What each person may respond to is individual. All of the ideas we explored in Chapter 5 about what is brought to the situation are also applicable to the person with depression too.

Helping effectively involves learning to listen, communicate, understand and learn from the person with depression about what and how they may benefit from your support. I would encourage you to read all the ideas of how to help in the following chapters, but then feel free, in collaboration with the person you are supporting, to adapt, be flexible, be creative and mix and match – to find the most helpful, individualized way to help them.

DON'T GIVE UP

Before we even describe the other skills and strategies, please hold on to this message: Don't give up. The depression may make the person you are helping feel like giving up. It may make you feel that way too at times. It can make you feel heavy, hopeless, frustrated and unable to see how things will get better. Remember, these will all be feelings the person with depression will be having too. This is part of the depression, part of the messages it sends. Yet please hold on to hope. Know that depression can change, get easier. Know that there are interventions that can help. Know that people can recover from depression. So please don't give up. Make sure you are supported – that is essential – and you may need to take a break as needed (we will talk about this further in Chapter 12) – but as far as you can, keep believing, sharing your hope for change with the person you are helping and keep offering support too.

REMEMBER: THIS IS THE DEPRESSION

Understand when a person is consumed with negative thoughts, emotions, behaviours and other symptoms, this is the depression. It is not, fundamentally, who the person is. This is how they appear, feel, think and behave when the depression has its grip. Without the depression, they would not think or feel this way and they would exist as the person you have always known them to be.

HAVE REALISTIC EXPECTATIONS

It is important for you, and also for the person you are helping, to have realistic expectations about their progress. To know that depression is a winding road of a journey where you may see 'progress' one day and more difficult days the next. It can help if you both know that it will not always be a smooth uphill trajectory of progress/recovery. Knowing that we cannot put a clear timeline on when the depression may fully lift is important too.

SHOW YOU CARE

No matter how many times you do this, it will always be immensely valuable to let the person you are helping know that you love them, that you care, that you will be there for them, that they matter whether the depression is present or not. You could show this through what you do, and/or what you say. Remember that because of the depression, they are likely receiving an endless stream of negative thoughts, which will include assumptions about what you think of them. Every time you can show them that they matter, that you want them to be here, that you love them, it will be a soothing antidote to the terrible thoughts the depression sends. Whilst the depression may make them struggle to believe your words, your messages will help give them an alternative narrative.

"Every time you can show them that they matter, that you want them to be here, that you love them, it will be a soothing antidote to the terrible thoughts the depression sends."

DEALING WITH OTHER MENTAL HEALTH ISSUES

Alongside the depression, the person you are helping may have other mental health issues – for example, anxiety, substance misuse, psychosis, eating disorders or self-harm. It is beyond the scope of this book to cover these in detail, but do seek advice, information and help with these as needed.

DO NOT UNDERESTIMATE THE IMPACT OF STIGMA

There remains a lot of stigma around mental health issues, including depression. For some people, families or cultures, this is more powerful than others. It can bring shame, which is an incredibly powerful and paralyzing emotion, and prevent a person from being open, honest, seeking help and sharing their full experiences. This may be a barrier and it is important to look out for it.

BE AWARE OF THE DEPRESSION–HONESTY CONFLICT

When a person experiencing depression is asked how they are, they may face a conflict about how honest they can be, especially when depression has been ongoing for a while. They can either:

a. Tell the truth about the difficult thoughts and feelings they are enduring, and the hopelessness about the future, but with the fear that the person they are talking to will be judgemental, overwhelmed, critical or be driven away.
   OR

b. Say 'I'm fine', provide an 'I'm better' pretence, and engage in a more superficial conversation, whilst internally feeling more lonely and desperate at how they know they truly feel.

Question: *'How are you?'*
Answer: *(I'm sad; I'm hurting; I'm scared; I can't sleep; I'm overwhelmed; I'm so worried; I can't bear it; I'm numb; I'm no good; No one cares; I'm alone.)* *'I'm fine.'*

Providing a supportive non-judgemental space, asking thoughtful questions about how a person is really doing, showing you are there to listen so they can be truly honest, safe in the knowledge that you will still be there for them, can be so incredibly valuable.

CHAPTER 7

WHAT TO SAY AND HOW TO SAY IT

When you are supporting someone with depression, it can be hard to find the right words, to know what to say. You might feel scared of saying the wrong thing. You might feel at a loss at what to say, or even where to start. You might find you can't seem to get it right.

This chapter will give you some ways to communicate with the person you are helping, including how to talk about the depression itself, because how we talk about it is important too. It can make a big difference to how you both relate to the experience of the depression.

We will explore:

1. How to talk about identifying and agreeing that this is depression
2. How to talk about 'the depression'
3. How to talk to the person with depression

IDENTIFYING THIS IS DEPRESSION

If the person you are supporting understands that this is depression, or they have already explored this with a health or medical professional, you can skip forward to how to talk about the depression (see page 99). If not, please read on.

If you have noticed a person is struggling, even if you aren't sure what is wrong (and don't assume you know for sure that it is depression), don't be afraid to talk about it.

Find a time to focus on the person and how they are, at a time when they will be most able to focus on themselves too. Let them know you have noticed they don't seem themselves and you are worried about them. Ask them how they are. If they say, 'I'm fine', carefully, gently wonder, 'Do you really feel you are? It seems like things are tough right now. Do you mind if we talk about it?' Or 'Do you have someone you can talk to?'

Open up the conversation to give them the best chance to talk. Gently, and with permission, explain what you are seeing, how things seem different and the symptoms you are noticing. Just this conversation alone can be powerful as the person may not have the insight yet to see the depression.

If you feel there are clear signs of depression, you might let them know specifically what you have noticed. Explain how you wonder if this may be depression and then listen to their response.

If the person is willing and ready, you could encourage them to complete a self-report questionnaire (see page 10 and Resources). Or you could try reading about depression together to see what they think, or suggest booking an appointment with a professional.

Be prepared for any of the following:

- The person you are supporting may not yet be ready to acknowledge their struggle or that there is depression present. They may have a different view.
- What looks like depression to you, might not be. This is OK. We can never truly know exactly what the experience is for someone else, so we have to trust and respect the person's views about themselves. And if a diagnosis is needed, then it is best for a professional to make it. But if you are noticing something is wrong, or you are worried, don't be afraid to have the conversation. Just aim to have this gently and kindly with compassion and without making assumptions.
- This conversation may take time – days, weeks, months even. A person may need time to process what you are saying, to consider it.

- If the person is experiencing depression, they may still reject this conversation, possibly because of shame, fear or stigma. Gently explore that. Are they worried about stigma? Being labelled? What are their fears? What are the barriers to seeking help? Some people have fears of how a disclosure of depression will impact their life.

"We can never truly know exactly what the experience is for someone else, so we have to trust and respect the person's views about themselves."

Whatever the response, don't give up hope, and don't underestimate the power of just having the conversation. For people at the milder end of the depression spectrum (see page 8), it may be part of the lift needed to begin to make changes themselves, even if you don't see it. For people at the severe end of the depression spectrum, the conversation will hopefully give them a chance to acknowledge how they feel and that they need help. The more severe the depression, the more important it may be to encourage and support the person to seek outside help, as this is a heavy burden to carry alone.

HOW TO TALK ABOUT 'THE DEPRESSION'

Research into the use of language has shown us that how we talk about 'a problem' makes a difference to how we perceive it, relate to it and tackle it. Narrative therapy approaches particularly emphasize how the language and narratives we use can be very powerful. Applying this to depression, how we talk about it can make a big difference to how we understand and cope with it, which is important for both you and the person you are helping.

Firstly, it can help to talk about depression as separate to the person. There is the person that you know and love, and there is 'the depression'. In narrative therapy this is called 'externalizing the problem'. It helps both you, and the person experiencing depression, to place the 'problem' outside of them. This makes it much easier for you both to look at it, face it, talk about it, and figure out how to tackle it and cope with it. When you talk about 'the depression', you help the person to see the depression as something separate, rather than seeing it as something inherently 'wrong' within them. Using externalizing language like this can be very powerful, non-judgemental and non-blaming.

Talking about the depression as separate to the person is especially useful when talking about the different symptoms of depression – for example, the negative, self-critical thoughts.

- The person with depression may say, 'I feel terrible, I'm such a failure, I can't even do X right, everyone is so much better at X than me...'. And you can be empathic and kind, and also notice, 'It must be so hard for you. It sounds like the depression is saying some really mean/cruel/bullying things to you today' or 'It sounds like the depression is being a real bully today. Is it like that all the time? It sounds so critical/unkind/horrible...'

- Another example of this is when the depression is making it hard to get out of bed, to face seeing people, to eat, to go to work. You can name this in your language: 'It sounds like the depression is making it feel really hard to do X today...' This helps the person experiencing depression (and you) to keep in mind that this is the depression having its impact rather than internalizing the symptoms as personal failures.

- The person you are helping may use descriptive imagery to describe the depression. For example, people talk about depression as the 'black dog', a 'dark cloud', 'a heavy storm', like 'being in a deep hole'. When talking to the person you are helping, you could say, 'I can't imagine what this must feel like and be like. What does this depression feel like for you?' If they have their own metaphors/descriptions/language, you can use these together.

- Once you know their description, you can ask questions using their language – for example, 'How is the depression storm today?', 'Can you see any light in the tunnel today?' You can use descriptor words: 'Is the depression quieter, lighter, louder, more bullying today?', or 'Is it feeling very heavy?' This approach helps you find a shared language, a shared way of talking about what a person is dealing with, which can be really valuable and meaningful.

"Talking about the depression as separate to the person is especially useful when talking about the different symptoms of depression."

HOW TO TALK TO THE PERSON

When talking to someone experiencing depression, you may find the following ideas and principles helpful.

OFFER COMPASSION AND EMPATHY

When a person is experiencing depression, they are living with a situation that brings them distress, mental torment, emotional pain; a situation that makes getting out of bed difficult, daily activities exhausting, conversations or decisions overwhelming.

Being able to offer compassion and empathy throughout someone's depression journey is an incredible gift. It helps the person know you have listened and have understood, or are trying to understand how they feel. It can help them feel seen, acknowledged, supported and cared for, which in turn will help them to begin to listen to the depression less and to trust more in the help and support that you can offer. Modelling compassion can also help them to consider being more self-compassionate to themselves.

HOW TO HELP

Here are some suggestions for how to respond in a compassionate and empathic way:

- 'I'm so sorry you are going through this.'
- 'It must feel so hard to hear the depression in your head like this.'
- 'It sounds incredibly hard. Can you tell me more about it, so I can understand?'
- 'I can't imagine what this must be like.'
- 'Living with depression in your life must be so very tough. I want you to know how amazing you are despite what the depression says.'

- 'I hope you know that you matter and you are worth so much, even if the depression is telling you something different.'
- 'Please take your time and know that I'm not going anywhere.'
- 'Thank you for trusting me with this/talking to me about how you feel.'
- 'I can hear how painful this feels. I am so sorry you have to experience this.'
- 'I hate that you are having to go through this. I wish I could make this OK for you.'
- 'I'm always here for you.'

Maintaining compassion and empathy is not always easy when you are in the helping role. It is common to struggle at times, especially as the depression lingers on. This can be known as 'compassion fatigue'. If you are struggling, please be kind to yourself and know this is a common response in the face of the challenges depression brings. See Chapter 12 on the importance of your own self-care to help you through this.

BE READY TO LISTEN

The person with depression may feel overwhelmed and be struggling to see things clearly. Offering the space and time to listen, to connect with them, so that they can talk and feel heard can be a huge gift. Most importantly, it is about *listening and hearing*, not (yet) about problem-solving or anything else. Just being able to be there to listen and understand is very powerful.

HOW TO HELP

Here are some ways to really listen to what someone is saying.

- Give the person your full attention, make eye contact, put your phone down, don't do another task at the same time.
- Try not to interrupt.
- Try not to jump in with examples from your own life or stories of your own – concentrate on the person who is talking.
- Think about your non-verbal communication – do your body and facial expressions show you are interested and listening or do they show you are bored, restless, uncomfortable and want to finish the conversation?
- Be OK with silence – allow the person time to speak if they are struggling to find words or are emotional. Give them time. You may need to sit quietly while they find their words or take a breath or calm/soothe

themselves. You can use gentle verbal encouragement, such as 'You are doing really well. Thank you for sharing this. Can you tell me more? It's OK I'm here, take your time... I'm listening.'

- When appropriate, ask gentle and curious questions about what they have just told you, or summarize what they have said (e.g. 'So it sounds like it feels really overwhelming. Is that right?' or 'It sounds like the depression is saying really mean things right now. What is it telling you?' This shows you have been listening and enables you to understand more.

"Just being able to be there to listen and understand is very powerful."

DON'T IGNORE THE DEPRESSION

Don't minimize, dismiss, ignore or pretend the depression isn't there. It can be very painful if the depression becomes the elephant in the room; something no one wants to talk about or mention. Or, even worse, if the person feels they are not believed. It can make them feel:

- Unheard, unseen, unsupported and uncared for
- Desperate, sad and angry
- That there is something wrong with them, which can't be talked about
- That they are only wanted/acceptable when they are 'happy'

So, it is important not to ignore the depression, or to only want to see or talk to the person when depression is not part of that picture, as this sends a very painful message. It is also very important to believe someone if they say they are experiencing depression or depression symptoms.

Of course, the person may want to talk about something other than the depression, and that is absolutely OK and can be really helpful and important. But try to always make sure you check in and ask about how the person is, how the depression is, to see if they want to talk about it.

"It can be very painful if the depression becomes the elephant in the room; something no one wants to talk about or mention."

SUPPORTER BURNOUT

It is, of course, important to acknowledge that if you have been supporting someone for a while and you have had many conversations about the depression, you may become burnt out, tired and worn down by talking about it.

If this is the case, it is important to look after yourself and, of course, to put yourself first. And at the same time, see if you can let the person with depression know you are still thinking of them.

Using the shared language of depression, you can talk together about how hard it is when depression is in your lives, how much it wears you both down. You can say that you know how tired *you* are feeling, so you can only begin to imagine how hard it is for *them*.

If you need a break, you could say, for example, that you are feeling a little overwhelmed or worn out right now and need to take a bit of time to recharge. If necessary you can explain this as feeling overwhelmed *with the depression*, not with the person themselves (however tread carefully with explaining this, as the depression will take any opportunity to make the person feel bad). Explain you are sending all your love and support, and you want to know how they are doing, because you know how incredibly tough this is, and you will check in with them. Then take some time out to do something relaxing and soothing for you. It is OK to have these conversations and take this time. Do this with love, care, compassion and honesty.

If you are concerned about issues of risk (see Chapter 4) then please see if you can enlist the help of other areas of the support system either personal (friends/family) or professionals to ensure they are aware you are taking a break and so they can step up to help.

ASK FOR PERMISSION TO HELP

It is important to be respectful and ask the person for permission to provide help, advice and support. The person with depression may mostly want to be heard, and to have the space to talk, rather than needing or wanting any kind of practical solutions. They may also not feel ready for help or advice – often it is just not the right time.

It is a natural instinct to want to make it better for someone, but when we rush in to try to fix, to give advice, share ideas or problem-solve, we can miss truly understanding what a person is going through. We can miss the opportunity to help the person figure out what they really need and to move toward it.

Offering unsolicited advice without permission can also make the depression even bigger and the emotions even more intense. Even if your help and advice is offered with all the best of intentions, unsolicited it may make a person feel:

- Not heard, not listened to and not understood
- Defensive or annoyed that advice is being given that doesn't feel useful at that time
- Judged or that you have missed the point
- That they don't want or need solutions (which they may already know or could think up themselves) – what they want is to be heard with empathy and care
- A failure and more alone

"When we rush in to try to fix, to give advice, share ideas or problem-solve, we can miss truly understanding what a person is going through."

HOW TO HELP

After listening, sitting with the emotions and acknowledging how the person feels, ask permission to help, with something like:

- 'I love you and I want to help. What can I do?'
- 'I'm so sad you are going through this. Can I suggest something to see if you think it might help?'
- I can see how hard things feel right now. Is there anything that you've found helps when you feel this way?'
- 'I am worried about you. I can see how hard things feel. Please can I help? I'd really like to. Perhaps I could help you with X or Y?'

BE OPEN TO ALL WAYS OF COMMUNICATING

There are so many ways we can communicate with others to show we love and care. We can meet in person and talk. We can phone, we can write letters and cards, we can text, we can email, we can send messages on social media, we can send photos and videos and audio messages, we can Zoom and FaceTime. We can send flowers and gifts. We can leave food parcels.

So, when a person is experiencing depression, be open to communicating with them in whatever way feels OK for them. They might have a preference for one type of communication – ask them. Some people prefer text, some prefer phone. Some might open up more in person. Notice how the person you are helping communicates with you and try to follow their lead. You could surprise them with a card or gift left on the doorstop to show you care. Be open to using ways to communicate that you are thinking of them, without them needing to reply, as communicating can become overwhelming when experiencing depression.

"Notice how the person you are helping communicates with you and try to follow their lead."

KEEP COMMUNICATING

Keep in contact. Be there. Be available. Not 24/7, but on a regular basis. You need to have your own time and your own boundaries, but don't let the depression fool you into thinking it is the right thing to step away. Depression can make a person want to push everyone and the world away, which can make communicating really hard. Don't give up. Don't take it personally. You are communicating with someone through the fog of depression.

A person experiencing depression will overthink every step. It will make replying to a text and holding a conversation really hard. It's not because you don't matter or they don't want to hear from you, it's because the depression is making it overwhelming.

The person may also have a number of people checking in on them, as well as obligations to maintain communications for work or social activities, and this can feel really overwhelming. They can easily get caught in a cycle of receiving messages, knowing they should reply, feeling so overwhelmed by the depression that they don't, and then experiencing guilt, shame, and more self-criticism that feeds back into the depression.

If you live with the person you're supporting, allow space and time to talk. Let them know you are there for them. Be OK to sit with them, without talking if they need quiet. Check in to see how they are doing or what they need. Understand they may not always have the words.

If you do not live with them, you can communicate via visiting, phone, post, email, text or social media. All you need to do is let the person know you are thinking of them. Keep in touch. Encourage them not to be alone for long periods. At the same time, do not expect anything from them or bombard them. Keep the pressure off. Just let them know you are there and thinking of them. Let them know you will check in again. Keep checking in.

The only caveat to this is if you are concerned about risk and cannot get hold of the person. In this instance, you may need to be persistent in getting a response. Don't be afraid to say: 'I am really worried about you. Please reply to let me know you are OK.' Take further action if needed. See Chapter 4 for responding to risk.

Do what you can to let them know you are there. Try, however, to avoid leaving things open-ended for the person to contact you. For example, avoid saying, 'I'm here if you need me' and then waiting to hear from them, as the chances are they won't initiate asking for support/company. You can, of course, say, 'I am here if you need me' and then suggest specific ideas to encourage connection or continue to contact them regularly to check in.

HOW TO HELP

Here are some ways to encourage connection:
- 'Could I come and make you a cup of tea?'
- 'Could I pop by and say hi on the doorstep?'
- 'I'm going for a walk today. Would you like to come?'
- 'Just letting you know I am thinking of you. Would you like to chat?'
- 'Just letting you know I am here and I will check in again later – no pressure, just respond when you can...'

BE HONEST AND OPEN

Don't be afraid to talk about how you feel. You can be open and honest, but also always be kind with this. There is a fine line between sharing how you are feeling (which the depression may then add to the person's burden), and hiding the impact of the depression on you (which is not healthy either). This is not an easy line to tread.

What can help is to think about your motivations and how the conversation can help you both. Sharing how you feel can be important for your relationship and help open up conversations about change, about how things can get better.

If you are sharing how you feel because you are (understandably) feeling frustrated and need to offload, perhaps think about other ways you can do this – perhaps talk to other parts of your support network.

If you are sharing how you feel because you really want things to get better, you are feeling overwhelmed with how things are, *and* you are holding on to the understanding this is the depression (not the person), it is OK to have this conversation kindly and gently. For example, you could say, 'I'm so tired, I'm finding the depression so hard. I don't feel like I'm helping, which makes me feel hopeless and frustrated. Things feel quite stuck. Maybe we need more help. What do you think?'

THINK ABOUT YOUR WORDS

The words you choose to communicate will be powerful. Remember the depression puts everything through a negative filter, including what the person hears from you. Be mindful of the words you use. Do your words suggest support or judgement? Do they suggest kindness or criticism? Do they convey empathy or irritation? Do they encourage or indicate disappointment?

Be gentle, thoughtful and kind. Remember you are talking to the person you care about, but you are talking through the filter of depression and you are talking about the depression. If you are feeling frustrated, weary and sad, remember to talk about feeling weary with *the depression*, not the person. Keep a mindful eye on anything you say that may:

- Inadvertently reinforce the depression
- Invalidate the person's feelings
- Be critical or may suggest they just aren't trying hard enough

"Remember the depression
puts everything through a negative
filter, including what the person
hears from you."

HOW TO HELP

Be aware of what *not* to say:
- 'If you just tried more...'
- 'Why can't you just...?'
- 'If you just do X, you'd feel better...'
- 'If you smile, you'll feel better...'
- 'Look on the bright side...'
- 'If you just think positively...'

- 'Everything happens for a reason...'
- 'Oh, when I feel sad, I just do X and I'm OK...'
- 'Are you *still* feeling depressed?'
- 'There are people dealing with lots worse... everyone hates their work/uni/studies at some time... life is stressful for everyone...'
- 'You're so selfish' (or other critical comments)
- On seeing the person smiling/laughing: 'I'm so glad you are better now' or 'You looked like you were having such a good time, you must be feeling better.' Unfortunately, these comments make a person powerless to say how they really feel. The person may be laughing and smiling and still feel dreadful inside, or have good moments, but still be hooked into the depression's grip moments later.

CHAPTER 8

EMOTIONAL SUPPORT

A person with depression will experience a wide range of emotions, such as sadness, anger, anxiety, panic, guilt, shame, loss and irritability. Sometimes the emotions may be subtle and sometimes they may be big and loud and distressing to observe. It can be difficult to know how to respond, as well as how to manage your own emotional and behavioural responses.

NAMING THE EMOTION

There is evidence that naming emotions can make them more tangible and, as a result, it can be easier to find a way to cope with or tolerate them. Helping the person name their emotions will also help you understand more about how they are feeling and what they are dealing with. It can also help to ask where they feel this in their body to help build their awareness of how they are experiencing this emotion. You can help to do this by asking them questions (see below).

HOW TO HELP

Here are examples of questions you could ask to help the person name their emotions:
- 'How are you feeling?'
- 'It sounds like the depression might be making you feel angry/anxious/scared/frustrated. Is that correct?' (Choose the emotion you think best describes how the person seems to be feeling.)
- 'I can't imagine what this must feel like. What are you feeling right now? Do you feel this physically in your body?'
- 'I can imagine it might feel really scary/lonely/sad. Is that how it feels?'

SITTING WITH EMOTIONS

When a person is experiencing one or more of the many emotions of depression, you can help enormously by just being able to 'sit' with the feeling and helping them sit with it too. This means listening to what the person is feeling, where they are feeling it in their body, bearing witness to it, acknowledging it, being with them despite the feelings, and staying calm in the emotional storm.

"Being able to sit with someone through their emotions is a powerful gift."

It can help the person to know that you are there and that you can bear their emotions, their distress, as this helps them to bear it too. They will feel that they can be honest and open about how they are feeling, not hide it or bury it. It can help for them to know there is nothing wrong with them for feeling what they feel or with the intensity they feel it. Being able to sit with someone through their emotions is a powerful gift.

BEING OK WITH BIG EMOTIONS

There will be times when the emotions will be big, intense and distressing, such as panic, deep sadness, despair and fear. It will be hard for you to see and sit with these emotions, but it can help immensely if you can stay calm and grounded, to be able to let the emotions rise and wash over you both, to hold on to the knowledge that the emotions will always move, pass, rise and fall, and that the intensity will die away again. If you offer a calm, compassionate space for the person experiencing depression, you will see this happen, and the emotions slowly come down in intensity. Trust in the process.

To help you further, as you read on in this chapter you will find specific ways you can help a person deal with very intense emotions.

YOUR OWN SELF-CARE

It is, of course, very difficult to bear witness to big, painful emotions and it is important to look after yourself. If you need to, you can tell the person that you feel a little overwhelmed, that it is hard for you to see them in pain and distress. Try taking a deep breath or use a grounding exercise (see Resources). Let them know if you need a minute to take time out for yourself. Step outside if you need and take a moment. If you do this, remember to always come back to finish the conversation and remind the person that you care and that you are there to support them.

You may want to seek support for yourself either through friends/family or with a professional to talk about the impact of these emotions on you. See also Chapter 12 for more on self-care.

ALLOW SPACE TO LET
THE EMOTION JUST BE

It can be tempting when we are faced with difficult emotions to:

- Form a judgement about them (e.g. 'What are they feeling like that for?', 'They don't need to feel this way', 'This is an overreaction/being dramatic')
- Want to fix and problem-solve, to convince the person they don't need to feel the way they do

The problem with this approach is that: a) when we form a judgement about a person it may stop us really listening and understanding how they are feeling; b) it won't change how the person with depression is feeling; and c), given that in the moment, most people don't want their emotions fixed or problem-solved and, given that attempts at persuading people they shouldn't feel what they feel are usually futile, they are likely to resist, defend and reject your solutions. They may then feel an increased level of distress at being unheard or not understood or supported.

In Chapter 9 we talk about how to provide practical help and support, as this is of course important at the right time, but the starting point is to be able to witness the emotion that comes with depression – aim to be there, to listen, without trying to solve it or change it in some way. Let the emotion be present, following the steps you have already learnt so far: notice the emotion, help name it, sit with it and let it rise and fall, respond empathically, compassionately and supportively, and don't rush in to dismiss or fix it.

> "If you want to help, you have to listen to how a person is really feeling. When I feel utterly depressed, or I'm having thoughts about not being here anymore, I don't want to be told that I just need to go out for a walk, have a warm drink or take a bath. It is like telling someone dying on the floor from a heart attack to just get up and take a walk. You wouldn't do this. You would sit with them and take care of them. When I feel like this, I want someone to sit with me, maybe give me a hug. Sometimes I don't want to talk, I just want someone to be there."
>
> Katie, aged 18

RESPONDING TO COMMON EMOTIONS

In the following pages I have provided some specific ideas of possible ways to respond to some of the common emotions in depression, drawing on the principles set out already in this chapter.

SADNESS/TEARFULNESS

The person with depression may feel sad for how life currently is, or sad about the past and/or the future. They may feel sadness at the negative thoughts the depression is telling them about themselves and about what others may be thinking of them. They may feel unable to cope with daily life. This sadness can weigh very heavily and they might often be tearful – it can be heartbreaking to witness.

- Help them recognize and acknowledge how they are feeling (name the emotion and where they feel it in their body). You can either let them talk and ask about how they are, or you could say something like, 'It looks like the depression is making you feel really sad right now. Is that how you are feeling? Where do you feel this in your body?' (E.g. it might be a lump in the throat, a heaviness in the chest.)
- Give them time to talk about how they are doing and what might be making them feel this sadness today.
- Offer compassion and empathy: 'I am so sorry the depression is making you feel this way. It breaks my heart to see you so sad.'
- Offer kindness, love, care and support as an alternative voice to the depression. An example might be: 'No

matter what the depression tells you, I want you to know you will get through this, even if the depression tells you otherwise. I know it is hard not to listen to what the depression is telling you, but I want you to know it is not being truthful or kind, and whatever it says I am here for you...'

- Ask their permission for the support you want to offer and allow them to choose. For example: 'Would you like a hug?'/'Is it OK for us to talk about this?'/'Can I sit here with you?'/'Do you want me to stay with you, or give you a bit of space for a while?'

- With permission, once you have listened, sat, offered kindness, empathy, physical comfort or given space, you can then try to gently open up the conversation to see if there is something that could help right now, whether that is listening more, talking about other things or doing something practical to help (see Chapter 9).

IT'S OK TO CRY

Be OK to sit with them in the quiet and let them cry. For some people there can be negative connotations with crying (e.g. 'I'm weak if I cry'), and so letting the person experiencing depression know it is OK, letting them express how they feel and letting them show their sadness and their tears, can be very powerful and supportive.

It can be tempting to want to help by saying, 'Please don't cry' or to try to help them stop the tears, but this can give the message that it isn't OK to cry, which we don't want to send. Instead offer kind words ('I'm so sorry for what you are going through'), and kind touch (e.g. a hug or holding their hand if they give permission for this) and let them express how they feel.

ANXIETY

Anxiety can grip a person experiencing depression. It can make them worry about daily life, second-guess everything, ruminate, overthink, question every decision and make it hard to focus. There may be physical symptoms of anxiety (upset stomach, aches and pains, tension, quickened heart rate/breathing, an uncomfortable feeling in the throat). The behavioural impact of anxiety can make the person with depression seek reassurance, get stuck on the same topics, or avoid people, activities and places. As this loop of symptoms gets stuck on repeat, it can feel frustrating. It may cause *you* anxiety, create irritation or even lead to avoidance of the person with depression.

• Support the person to name and acknowledge the emotion that is present (in this case feeling 'anxious' or 'worried' – use their words) and where they feel this in their body.

- Let them talk about what is making them feel anxious.
- Offer compassion/empathy/understanding. An example might be: 'It sounds like you are feeling really anxious right now. It must be so tiring with all this buzzing round your mind.' Or: 'I know anxiety can really affect how you feel in your body which can feel really difficult to rest or relax.'
- Gently remind them it is the depression: 'It sounds like the depression is making you feel really anxious.'
- You could say: 'I can hear you feel really anxious. Is there anything that you know would help right now?' (The person may be able to pause and think about what they know helps and you can help them with that – it may be something from the list below. If they suggest anything, follow their lead as a first step.)
- Ask permission to offer them ideas to help them calm and soothe – you could let them know these exercises are designed to help calm the physical symptoms in the body and help the mind rest too:
  o Take some slow, deep breaths – you could do this together.
  o Try a relaxation exercise or meditation – there are many online.
  o Go for a walk or do some other sort of exercise.
  o Have a relaxing bath.

o Use a scented candle or scent stick

o Do some yoga.

UNHELPFUL SOOTHING STRATEGIES

It is possible the person may suggest/choose to turn to alcohol or drugs to help themselves calm and soothe. We know that whilst people may initially feel better for making this choice, they can often end up feeling more anxious after choosing these strategies (e.g. a person who has several drinks may wake up feeling more anxious the next day) and of course these are known to be unhelpful coping strategies for the wider effects that they can have on a person. So it can help to gently have this conversation, and see if they would consider trying some other approaches with you instead. You can say: 'I know it must feel really tempting to open that wine now, but I know you've also said it makes you feel worse in the morning. Could we try something else? We could find something that we could try together.'

- With permission, help them problem-solve their worries:
  o First, ask: 'Would it help if we worked through the things you are worrying about? We could try to figure these out together.'
  o Help them write a list of all the things they are worrying about.

- o Then work through each worry, seeing if there is anything practical they could do to solve the worry, and if so make a plan to do this.
- o Help them identify the worries that they can't do anything about. Help them acknowledge this, and that therefore worrying about this issue will only make them feel worse, but not make any difference to the outcome.
- o Help explore ways to let worries go. Mindfulness strategies are really useful for this (see Resources).
- o One of my favourite strategies for letting worries go is imagining the worries are written on balloons. Imagine letting each balloon go and letting it drift off into the sky. You can repeat this as many times as needed. Then gently refocus your attention onto a task that would be useful right now.

"Support the person to name and acknowledge the emotion that is present."

- If the person is repeating worries you have discussed previously, you could listen but also gently pause them and say something like: 'It sounds like the anxiety has got really big again today and is keeping you stuck in this loop of the worries we were talking about the other day. Would it help to remember what we talked through then?'

HOW TO RESPOND TO PANIC, OVERWHELM AND DISTRESS

It is possible, at times, for anxiety to become really big, for a person to feel overwhelmed and for panic to grow. In some cases, this sits as a simmering panic and in other cases can lead to a panic attack. Not everyone who becomes depressed experiences panic, but if the person you are supporting does, the following information may be useful.

A panic attack happens when a person's internal threat system gets overloaded by either external triggers (something happening in their environment) and/or internal triggers (thoughts, images, memories). The body begins to experience unpleasant physical symptoms (e.g. heart racing, throat constricting, difficulty swallowing, finding it hard to catch their breath, feeling hot, tingly, faint, dizzy). The symptoms can feel scary, which can feed into the panic cycle, but the important part is they cannot cause actual harm.

Some people with depression may experience other intense emotions that trigger them to feel extremely emotionally overwhelmed, agitated and distressed. This can be distressing for them and distressing for you to observe.

What the person most needs at this point is calm, focused support that will help to ground them. Here are some tips on how to do this:

- Stay calm – take deep breaths yourself if you need to.
- Try not to feed the distress/anxiety/panic by saying too much – you want to be a calm, soothing, grounding presence.
- Offer reassurance by saying something like, 'I'm here. It's going to be OK. I'm with you, breathe with me...'
- If the person is breathing fast, say the above kindly but firmly, using their name. For example, 'Ellen, I can see this feels overwhelming. I want to help. Just breathe with me, you're going to be OK, just focus on me, breathe in, slowly; now breathe out.' Say this slowly with pauses to help them slow down. And repeat. You can add counting if this helps: 'Let's breathe in for three counts – 1, 2, 3, hold for a moment. Now let's breathe out – 1, 2, 3.' Count slowly. Breathe with them so they can see and hear you taking the slow breaths and can follow your lead. It can also help to ask them to put a hand on their stomach and to try to push out as they breathe in. This helps them really fill their lungs with deep breaths.
- Try to gently orientate them to you. Use their name: 'Seb, I'm here. Seb, can you look at me? Could you hold my hand?'
- You can also gently orientate them to the room and the present: 'Daniel, can you focus on this picture on the wall? Tell me what you can see, tell me something you can hear right now.'

- Give them space to pace and move around if they need. Don't go into their personal space – they will be feeling overwhelmed and it can be threatening.
- Ask them to sit with you when they are ready. Quietly be with them as they settle.
- Be confident in the belief that this emotional storm will pass. You can be a strong, calm, gentle anchor in the storm.
- When things are calm, you can explore what they think triggered their distressed or panicked response, so you can support them if it happens again. You could suggest learning a breathing or grounding exercise or listen to one together. See Resources.

"You can be a strong, calm, gentle anchor in the storm."

HOW TO RESPOND TO ANGER AND IRRITATION

Anger and irritation may particularly manifest itself in depression in men (see page 16), but it can show up for anyone. When a person is struggling to sleep, is fatigued, heavy with emotion, bombarded with negative thoughts, finding it difficult to focus, think straight or organize themselves because of the depression, then it is possible to see how anger and irritability can grow. You might notice the anger or irritability directed at you, at children, friends, family members, colleagues or people in the community.

- Stay calm.
- Try to notice your own emotional/behavioural responses. You may feel cross, defensive or irritated in response to a person's anger or irritation. It is normal to feel defensive when on the receiving end of anger. However, if you can, take a breath and remember this is part of the depression.
- Remind yourself that when a person is angry, it is often masking other emotions underneath (e.g. sadness, worry, exhaustion, anxiety, grief, loss, fear). When you remember this, it is easier to be empathic and understand what might really be underneath their anger/irritability.
- Respond gently and kindly. At times it can be helpful to say as little as possible, rather than feed the anger/irritation.
- Try not to get into a disagreement about the content of the anger. Instead, try to talk to the anger itself and what is underneath it. Let the person know: 'I can hear/see you are feeling angry. You must be exhausted dealing with everything/with this depression. I want to help. I'm here. What can I do?'

HOW TO RESPOND TO NUMBNESS/ DISENGAGEMENT

One of the more difficult emotions depression can bring is numbness, feeling 'flat' or an absence of emotion. This can be difficult for the person experiencing depression and for those supporting them. It may appear that the person doesn't care, but this is very far from the truth.

Depression can also make a person appear disengaged and distant. Again, it may appear that they don't care, but actually it is most likely they are so overwhelmed with the internal symptoms of depression (the critical thoughts, the negative emotions, the physical sensations), that they are using up all their resources just to cope with those and, as a result, they have nothing left to engage fully with the outside world and their relationships. This makes them appear disconnected.

To try to engage with the person:

- Most importantly be kind and non-judgemental.
- Let them talk about how they feel (numb, flat, disconnected, distant) and acknowledge how hard that must be.
- Try not to take it personally. Remember, the person does care; they are just struggling at the moment.

- Accept they may be more distant right now or may struggle to express emotions apart from the numbness. Do not blame or criticize them for this. Remember, this is the depression.
- Look after yourself and seek help and support if you need to.
- Let the person know you understand how hard it must be to be present when the depression is like this. Let them know you understand these feelings are all part of the depression and you are hopeful that this will change. Let them know they are OK and loved however they are.
- Understand that whatever way they engage with you and others is all they can manage right now. They are doing their best. It will be difficult for both them and you.
- Keep encouraging them to participate and engage with you and others, gently and gradually, at their pace. Do not expect them to experience a big increase in pleasure or engagement immediately, but taking part is a great step.

CHAPTER 9

PRACTICAL SUPPORT

This practical chapter intentionally comes after the chapters on communicating and providing emotional support, because it is important that you explore those routes first. If you jump in too soon with practical advice, you may miss understanding what the person is feeling and what they truly need. This may leave them feeling like more of a problem to be solved rather than being truly seen, heard and cared for. You may also end up offering unhelpful or unwanted practical advice if you jump in too soon.

EMPOWER

It is important to provide support, but not do everything for the person you are helping. You want to demonstrate your belief in their ability to get better, to help themselves, and hold on to their own responsibility and own part in getting better. When you do too much, rather than supporting them to do things themselves, it can ultimately make it harder for them to move forward.

Doing things *together*, however, can be really helpful, especially when you are first looking at ways to help activate and motivate a person with depression. They may need support to get things started initially, especially when the depression has slowed them right down or completely stopped them. Having you (or a fellow supporter) there to do an activity with them may be immensely helpful (at least at first).

NOTICE WHAT HAS CHANGED

Depression affects how a person behaves. See if you can take a moment to notice how it has affected the person you know. What has the person started doing *less* of, avoiding, withdrawing from, since the depression took hold (e.g. reduced or stopped taking part in exercise, hobbies, socializing or self-care)? What has the person started doing *more* of, since the depression has taken hold, that might not be helping them, or might be keeping them stuck in the depression (e.g. drinking more, staying in bed, cancelling plans)?

Gently and kindly have a conversation with the person about these changes:

- Let them know what you have noticed, and see if they have noticed the same pattern.

- Ask if they think these changes are helping them feel better or worse overall.
- With permission, begin to think about how you could work toward helping them make changes for the better.
- What hobbies, interests or activities could they work toward restarting with support?
- What unhelpful new habits could they look at cutting down with support?
- Problem-solve and plan ways together that they could make changes and who could help with this.

DEPENDENCE ON ALCOHOL OR DRUGS

If a person is struggling with an increase in alcohol or drugs to cope with depression, you, or other parts of their support system (family/friends) may be able to help them reduce this or make changes if they are keen to do so and the use hasn't become too problematic. However, it may be that external support is needed from health professionals experienced in reducing or stopping the misuse of alcohol or drugs. You may need to have an honest conversation with the person with depression if you feel this is outside of the scope you can help with. Be aware that these conversations may take time as the person will need to be ready to seek help for these difficulties.

ENCOURAGE GETTING OUTSIDE AND EXERCISE

As a supporter of someone with depression, encouraging movement and exercise in a kind way that suits the person can be one of the most helpful strategies you can implement. To start with, getting them to go outside into the fresh air or nature, even it is just having a stretch, standing on the doorstep or having a cup of tea in the garden/balcony/street, can be hugely beneficial.

Studies have found benefits when a person with depression engaged in:

- Exposure to sunlight (safely)/vitamin D, especially in the mornings
- Being in nature
- Movement and exercise

Research has repeatedly found beneficial links between staying active and mental health, with evidence for the natural antidepressant effects of exercise. The National Institute for Health and Clinical Excellence (NICE) in the UK recommends exercise for helping people with depression.

HOW TO HELP

Encourage the person with any of these ideas for exercise and outdoor activity:

- Walking, including dog walking
- Jogging
- Yoga/Tai Chi
- Gardening
- Hiking
- Cycling
- Nature trails
- Coastal/river walks
- Having a cup of tea at a beauty spot
- Aerobics/keep fit/boot camps/HIIT (high-intensity interval training classes)/personal training
- Playing outdoor games, such as tennis, rounders, golf, football, cricket, catch and frisbee

Movement can be anything from a gentle walk to an intense run or workout. Try to make activities as easy and stress-free as possible for the person you are helping. Offer to meet them for a walk or drive them to a beauty spot. Suggest places where it is likely to be less busy, where they could wear their comfiest clothes and where they would be unlikely to bump into people. If they don't want to go somewhere, offer to take over a picnic that you can share together in their garden. Ask if they will support you with an activity (e.g. a Couch to 5k programme). Find a mutual cause (e.g. a fundraising walk for a charity). See if you could do something fun together, or something out of your comfort zones (e.g. book a paddleboarding or surf lesson, or try a fun-run – there are some races that have inflatable obstacles or colour runs that end up with you covered in multi-coloured dyes).

There are also benefits in 'walk and talk' activities, including mindful walking (see Resources). A person with depression may feel more comfortable with this as walking side by side involves less eye contact, a more relaxed setting, and all the advantages of fresh air and exercise. So, offering the space for them to talk whilst walking will be offering multi-level benefits.

When encouraging someone to move more with you or to get outside, you can be honest by saying something like, 'I'm worried about you, humour me. Please come and sit and have a cup of tea in the garden with me/come for a walk with me'. Encourage, support, gently nudge forward. And don't give up trying.

"Try to make activities as easy and stress-free as possible for the person you are helping."

"I came to exercise at a low point in my life. I was suffering from depression, I had issues with alcohol and my marriage had just broken down. I started running to help make a change, to get out of all the bad habits of drinking and crashing alone in front of the TV. Exercise quickly became a form of therapy for me, a chance to get out in the world, de-stress, and work out the anxieties and problems going round my head. Sweat brought back my smile, challenging myself through exercise brought me a purpose I was desperately missing from my life. When I feel low, it can be hard to motivate myself to get out, but I remember why I am doing it and I remind myself how good I feel when I've done it."

Guy Stapleford, cyclist, runner and fundraiser

SUPPORT SOCIAL INTERACTION

Research tells us that meaningful social interaction can help lift our mood when we feel low. This can start with small interactions, like small talk at the checkout in a shop or a chat with a friend, and progress to being part of a work meeting, online/virtual contact, attending dinner or drinks with friends, a family party. Even if it only lifts mood by one per cent, it can help a person feel less alone and more connected. However, it does need to be at a level that the person can tolerate, otherwise it can increase the sense of feeling overwhelmed or being alone in a crowd. Encouraging and providing opportunities for this is important, but also be open to listening to the level of meaningful social interaction a person can tolerate. Encourage in small steps but don't push too hard too soon or they may feel overwhelmed.

ENCOURAGE SELF-CARE

When depression becomes overwhelming, self-care becomes hard. Depression makes a person neglectful of themselves. This can range from stopping a previously active self-care routine (e.g. exercising, having a relaxing bath, meditating, doing yoga, healthy eating) to, at the more severe end of depression, stopping basic self-care (e.g. eating regularly, cleaning the house, washing the dishes, changing clothes, getting dressed, showering, brushing hair, making the bed). Encouraging a return to the currently neglected activities, without judgement, can be important and helpful. Talk with the person and pick one thing together that might feel manageable to them. Offer help and support to get started and to keep going.

> "Encouraging a return to the currently neglected activities, without judgement, can be important and helpful."

OFFER PRACTICAL HELP

Let the person know you are there for them, and then ask them what they need and how you can help. Don't assume, don't jump in with support that has not been asked for. The only caveat to this is being prepared for the fact that sometimes the person with depression may feel so overwhelmed that they don't know what they need. In which case you can ask permission to suggest some ideas.

Some people with depression (particularly, but not exclusively, at the more severe end) may be struggling with simple everyday practical tasks, such as cooking, shopping, washing, paying bills, cleaning and doing laundry, or there may be a high level of self-neglect. You could offer practical help by helping them tackle these tasks.

At the milder end of depression, a person may appear to be functioning, but they actually need help and support to rest, to stop, to do less, to prioritize some self-care, and you could offer support to enable this.

You could talk with the person and let them know you can see things are hard right now, and ask their permission to help. Be prepared that they may likely decline, or say they can manage. It is OK to not give up at offering help. You could say 'Please let me help. I want to help. I know this is a tough time and I want to be here for you.' Ask if or what practical help they might need and, if necessary, gently offer some ideas, such as:

- **Preparing a home-cooked meal and dropping it round:** Ideally prepare something that can be served in small portions and stored in the freezer or heated up easily. Large meals may feel overwhelming and unachievable if the person has no appetite, although they may be helpful for others in the household. You could also take round small and easy snacks/meals that the person may find more manageable.
- **Offering to help with shopping:** Ideas could include driving them to the shops at a time they feel able to go; seeing if they would prefer to go to a small store; sitting together and helping them order shopping online or via an app; letting them know you are in a shop and asking if they need anything.

- **Offering to help with housework:** If possible, do housework together, even if working together in silence or chatting together while you help or they sit with you.
- **Childcare:** If the person has young children, you could offer to look after them for an hour, pick them up from school, give them dinner or have them to play at weekends.
- **Organizing/managing:** Offer to sit together and go through their calendar/tasks and letters/bills so they can feel on top of this.
- **Pampering:** Offer to run a bath for them and make sure they have all the right toiletries and a clean towel.

"There were days when I couldn't get out of bed, couldn't face preparing food or eating. I didn't think I deserved to eat, and couldn't see the point anyway. Sometimes I just felt sick in my stomach. I was losing weight and I know now that everyone was worried. I didn't care about myself. My family cared, though. They would come over, and bring me soups, smoothies. They would find different things for me to try that I could stomach. Slowly I began to be able to eat a bit more again."
Rosie

ENCOURAGE ENGAGEMENT IN MEANINGFUL ACTIVITY

Where it is not leading to further deterioration, it is encouraged to keep going by continuing to attend school, college or work – on balance this is typically helpful for mood and wellbeing. If needed, however, this may be in reduced ways or with support. For example, it might involve liaising with tutors/teachers or colleagues/managers/occupational health to find ways to help the person, such as getting extra support, reducing targets or revising hours. It may also involve planning extra self-care activities for before or after school/work.

There is a fine line between taking time off due to depression and keeping attendance going despite the depression as part of recovery. Taking time off can sometimes leave a void, which the depression can take advantage of, leading to increased low mood. Therefore, at times, it is better to keep going as the benefits will outweigh the negatives.

There is, of course, a point when time off is required either because the person is significantly struggling to function, or because at the other end of the spectrum, some people with depression will continue to function but work too hard or study all hours. If you notice this, then providing encouragement and support to take some time off, to rest and recharge, can be essential.

GETTING THE BALANCE RIGHT

Sometimes we need to push and encourage a person to take part in an activity the depression is persuading them to avoid, because we know the research suggests it will make them feel a little better once they do so. However, sometimes we absolutely need to respect the need for peace, to rest and opt out.

It is important not to guilt or shame a person into doing something the depression is making them feel they cannot do. But also, not to get into a battle or become cross/frustrated if they do not feel they can manage the activity this time. Be open and honest about the fine line you are walking, the balance you want to help them achieve and see if you can find a way to tread this together.

> "Sometimes we absolutely need to respect the need for peace, to rest and opt out."

HOW TO HELP

Here are some ideas to encourage and be respectful of the space a person needs:
- Try saying something like: 'I hate trying to push you to do something you don't feel like doing, but I also don't

want to leave you here alone. It might help to try X? Or maybe we could choose something else to try instead. What do you think?'

- Find a compromise, by offering alternatives. Examples might be:
  - 'Can we sit and watch a film together, rather than you being in your room?'
  - 'Can we sit in the garden for a bit, rather than going for a walk?'
  - 'Could you try going into college/work for half a day if the whole day feels too much? Would the morning or afternoon be easiest?'

As a tentative rule of thumb, for the milder end of depression, it may be more important to encourage rest initially and briefly, but with the aim of re-engagement fairly quickly. At the more severe end of the spectrum, it may be more important to encourage engagement in activity in very small manageable steps.

THE RIGHT ACTIVITIES AT THE RIGHT LEVEL

It will be helpful for the person to take part in activities that bring a sense of achievement, enjoyment, pleasure or social connection. This is drawn from a psychological therapy approach called 'behavioural activation', which shows that engaging in such activities improves motivation and mood. Anything that you can do to support or encourage the person to consider (with permission and in collaboration with them) activities that may fall into these categories (which bring a sense of achievement or mastery, enjoyment or pleasure, or social connection) could be helpful. When supporting a person to re-engage with activities it can help to keep these principles in mind:

- The activity should be manageable.
- Any goals or targets should start small, and then gradually increase.
- Support the person with finding the right pace and level for them at this time.
- Encouragement to do a little more each time than the depression might tell them may be helpful. Look out for, recognize and praise any small steps forward.

"What has always helped me is to feel like I am doing something useful, taking care of and helping my family. I talked to my psychologist about what was important to me. I told her I loved gardening – being in my garden, seeing the roses, the flowers, the tomatoes growing. It has always made me happy. It's upsetting that I can't do as much now, but I liked being supported to see what I could still do. I could still help with planting if someone

helped put the pots in my reach. And I could let people know all the things I wanted in the garden or ask for help when I could see things needed doing. I also love cooking. We found ways for me to be involved in baking bread and looked at ways I could do the online shopping. I also kept doing my exercise class, doing my art, seeing my friends, and talking to my grandchildren online. These things didn't solve the depression, but they definitely helped me."

Geraldine

HOW TO STEP OUT OF THE DARKNESS

If the person you are helping is significantly struggling with day-to-day activities, such as self-care and interactions, you could ask their permission to show them the 15 small steps opposite.

If they agree, talk together about these steps and see if you can support them with one of these today, or more if they feel up to it. Let the person choose how many and which steps.

If they are struggling to choose, you could identify a couple of steps and ask them to pick one. Or ask if you can pick one for them. Ask them if you can do the step with them, or if they would like you to check in with them and help them in any way.

For anyone struggling with depression, don't expect them to achieve all of these steps in one go, but you can agree a place to start, together. Or you can leave these ideas with them to think about. If they find it helpful, you can listen and talk about the challenges that come up for them, in their mind, in their body, when they think about trying any of these, and see if you can help them overcome these challenges.

15 SMALL STEPS TO TAKE NOW

Support the person you are helping to try one or more of these small steps. Let them read each question and then think about what they could manage.

1. Have you had a drink of water today or a warm drink? Have one now.
2. Have you got out of bed today? Move back the covers and sit on the edge of the bed. Stand up, walk around your room, go into a different room of the house. Walk around the house.
3. Have you washed today? Splash some water on your face, take a shower or run a bath.
4. Have you dressed today? If you are still in your pyjamas, go to your clothes and choose something comforting, clean and fresh. Put this on now.
5. Have you brushed your hair today, put on scent/make-up, looked in the mirror kindly? Do this now.
6. Have you eaten something today? Eat a cracker, cereal, piece of fruit, biscuit, slice of bread, carrot. Take a bite of something now.

7. Have you taken a slow, deep breath today? Place a hand on your stomach. Pause. Breathe in slowly, breathe out.

8. Have you moved today? Stretch your arms, stretch them out to the side, up in the air; walk around, gently move your body.

9. Have you stepped outside today? Open the window, step into the garden, patio, on to the drive, into the street, on to the balcony, just for a moment. Breathe in the fresh air. See if you can feel the fresh air and stay there for ten seconds, a minute, five minutes.

10. Have you tidied up today? Give yourself five minutes to straighten up the room you are in.

11. Have you made your bed? Make your bed, straighten the covers so it is nice to get into at the end of the day.

12. Have you connected with someone today? Send one message or reply to one message on your phone.

13. Have you completed a to-do list task today? This could be putting the laundry on, emptying the bin, washing up, feeding the cat, sending an email, paying a bill, purchasing a gift for someone, booking an appointment, going to the local shop.

14. Have you done one thing today that brings you some light or peace? This could be watching a favourite movie, playing music, going for a walk, drawing, painting, cooking, having a bath, reading, gardening,

seeing a friend, having a cuddle, giving yourself permission to rest.

15. Have you been kind to yourself today? Place a hand on your heart and acknowledge, right now, this is really hard/painful/scary/overwhelming, yet you are doing this. One small step at a time.

WHEN TO SUGGEST OTHER SUPPORT

As you've seen from this chapter, there are many ways you can offer practical support, but there may be times when you can see the grip of the depression and feel that the person needs more help. You may want to talk together about the possibility of therapy or medication, or you may need more support for yourself. We will explore how to get professional support in Chapter 11.

"My therapy really helped me piece together a lot of my past to make me realize why I feel the way I do about certain things. I also take antidepressants. Quick wins are things like playing with my kids, but my biggest and most effective strategy is to get outside in the fields and woods to walk my dog. It's an opportunity to clear my head, speak out loud, breathe deeply and appreciate nature."

Jamie Day, mental health advocate, writer and podcaster

CHAPTER 10

SPECIFIC SCENARIOS

Sometimes when someone is struggling with depression, it can be difficult to know what to say and do in specific situations. In this chapter, you will find ideas for how to help with some common situations that often arise in depression. As with everything we have talked about, the exact way you can help will be individual to you and to the person with depression, so please be flexible in considering what feels right. For each of the scenarios, I encourage you to remember the following key approach which draws on the principles of Chapters 6 to 9:

R.E.L.A.T.E
- **R**emember this is the depression
- **E**mpathy, compassion, let them know they are loved
- **L**isten and acknowledge how hard this must be
- **A**sk permission before offering advice
- **T**ake a break, breathe, ground yourself as you need
- **E**ncourage and empower to take steps toward change

NOT GETTING OUT OF BED

Depression brings overwhelming feelings of lethargy, exhaustion, demotivation, physical aches and overwhelming self-critical thoughts that can feel paralyzing. It can make a person feel unable to get out of bed and unable to face the day. Cruelly, it can make getting out of bed feel impossible, whilst making sleep feel inescapable as well. At other times a person may stay in bed because sleeping is the only way to cope, block out or numb what they are feeling. As a general rule, the more severe the depression, the more significant this 'staying in bed' behaviour can be. The more severe this behaviour gets, the more likely it is to lead to self-neglect (see page 164).

HOW YOU CAN HELP

- Remember R.E.L.A.T.E (see page 155).
- If the person is in bed, ask permission to come in and see them, or offer to meet them outside/for a walk (to encourage them to get up). Don't be afraid to be fairly persistent and let them know you are worried about them and want to help.
- Encourage them to talk to you and listen to how they are feeling and how they describe the behaviour (e.g. what do they say about why they are staying in bed?). Listen,

empathize, sit with the emotion. Acknowledge how hard it must be to hear the depression in their mind; to feel the way they do; to feel unable to get up and function.

- Keep in mind there is a balance between allowing someone the space to process the depression in the way that they need (e.g. resting, taking some time out), versus the importance of encouraging strategies or behaviours that will help create more light and change the course of the depression (e.g. getting out of bed). Try to be open and honest about this dilemma: 'I can hear how hard it feels to get up, or how much you want to stay in bed right now, and I want to support you... but I am worried in case this makes the depression heavier or makes you think I/we/no one cares.'

- Let them know you are there for them and they are loved no matter what (to combat the very heavy voice of depression at this time).

- Let them know you are worried and ask if you could suggest some small steps that might help. For example: 'Could we just try something small?' Examples might be: sit up in bed, open the curtains, consider putting on some music or the radio, put the TV on, come downstairs in pyjamas, stand in the garden (in a dressing gown is fine), have a shower/bath, have a cup of tea or glass of water,

have a small snack, such as a piece of toast. Offer to help
them with anything they feel they can manage.

- Reinforce how proud you are of them for taking any small
steps. Thank them for giving it a go.

"Let them know you are there for them and they are loved no matter what."

- Don't pretend or assume that everything will suddenly be
better by taking any initial steps. Keep in mind the person
may feel under pressure to suggest it has helped when
they may still feel awful. Don't underestimate how loud
and heavy the depression can be.

- Let them go back to bed when they signal they need to.
Small steps are OK.

- See if you can gain agreement to try a similar set of steps
again a bit later that day or the next day. Again, gentle,
kind persistence may be necessary. How much will depend
on the severity of the depression.

UNDEREATING OR OVEREATING

When depression takes hold, appetite changes are common.
Depression may cause people to lose interest in food and
cooking; they may feel like they don't care about themselves

enough, or don't deserve food. Depression can also cause physical symptoms like constant nausea, which makes it harder to think about eating. Depression can also cause people to overeat, binge eat or secretly eat. Depression can cause intense negative emotions, which can lead people to engage in emotional overeating as a coping mechanism. Or overeating may be a way to self-sabotage themselves or to punish themselves.

Caution: If the person appears to have an eating disorder (anorexia, bulimia, binge-eating) as well as depression, seek professional support.

HOW YOU CAN HELP IF THE PERSON ISN'T EATING

- Remember R.E.L.A.T.E (see page 155).
- Don't be afraid to ask directly (and kindly, with concern) if they are eating. Say something like, 'Are you feeling like you are able to eat at the moment?'
- Ask if the depression is making them feel it is difficult to eat. Encourage the conversation to find out if the depression is telling them they don't deserve to eat, or that there is no point, or they just don't have the energy or appetite.
- Let them know that appetite changes are common in depression and whatever the depression is telling them,

they deserve to eat and eating will give them some energy to fight this depression.

- Talk together to find out what they might feel able to tolerate eating more easily – perhaps soups, smoothies, milkshakes, toast, crackers, cereal.
- If having the energy or motivation to shop or cook is the problem, get consent to bring foods, cook foods, or write a list/go out to the shops together to choose something they can face eating.
- Don't expect too much at first. Any small steps forward in eating are helpful. Don't express negativity if they don't finish everything. Praise any attempts to eat more.

"When depression takes hold, appetite changes are common."

HOW TO HELP IF THE PERSON IS OVEREATING/ EMOTIONAL EATING

- Remember R.E.L.A.T.E (see page 155).
- If the person brings it up, let them talk about how their mood is affecting their eating.
- If they are saying something like 'I am fat/lazy...', listen and see if you can help them re-label what the depression is telling them. For example, 'It must be so tough. The

depression is being really mean, telling you are fat/lazy, when actually you are struggling with depression.'

- Encourage them to see the situation for what it is: 'It sounds like you are feeling really overwhelmed because of the depression and when you feel that way you are eating more to cope with the feelings or craving more sugary foods. Did you know this is really common in depression? You are not alone in struggling with this.'

- Be understanding. Don't judge or show any negativity or disapproval about weight gain or overeating. If they are struggling with emotional overeating, or feeling shame about weight gain, being critical will only push them further into overeating.

- At this stage, supporting them with the depression itself is likely to be the most important problem that you can help them with. Eating issues will likely improve and be easier to deal with as mood improves. Don't focus on addressing the overeating/weight issue unless they ask you to help. Take the lead from the person with depression on this.

- However, if they do ask for help and support, ask what you can do. For example, do they want support with food ideas, menu planning, walks, or exercise together? Emphasize how this could help you too. Try to focus on how it can help the depression and wellbeing rather than there being any emphasis on weight gain/loss.

"Don't expect too much at first. Any small steps forward are helpful."

NOT SLEEPING

Depression disrupts sleep – there may be difficulty getting to sleep, staying asleep or early-morning wakening, or all three. It can cause restlessness at night, panic, anxiety, bad dreams, night terrors, intense worry/overthinking or dark negative thoughts. At night, emotions and thoughts are heightened and feel more intense. This makes things darker, heavier and more overwhelming. Insomnia is common. This can, of course, lead to fatigue, tiredness, irritability, emotional sensitivity and exhaustion in the daytime, and the person may begin to doze off at the time they need to be waking up. Sleep can be disrupted at all ends of the depression spectrum – from mild to severe.

HOW TO HELP

- Remember R.E.L.A.T.E (see page 155).
- Understand how depression affects sleep. You can offer to explain it to the person you are helping if they would find it useful.

- Check that the conditions for sleep are optimal. Some good sleep hygiene tips are:
    o Check that the room is warm/cool/dark enough.
    o Drink less prior to bedtime so that needing to get up to use the toilet does not contribute to night-time waking.
    o Make sure the bed and bedding are comfortable.
    o Don't do work in bed.
    o Try not to drink alcohol/caffeine, or exercise, too close to bedtime.
    o Limit blue light at night-time from screens on phones, iPads, computers etc.
    o Try to have a regular night-time wind-down routine and a regular bedtime.
    o Consider using relaxation aids – sleep masks, relaxing sleep sprays, weighted blankets, relaxing music, white noise apps, scents/candles, mindfulness apps.
- If the person with depression is struggling with nightmares and bad dreams, or is overwhelmed with negative thoughts and rumination at night, encourage them to consider seeking support for this. Therapy can focus on helping a person sleep better at night and help them manage negative or anxious thoughts. Therapy interventions can also help

address bad dreams and nightmares, even if the content of the dream isn't recalled (see Resources). Mindfulness approaches and apps also help.

- During the day, support the person with depression to talk about how they are doing and what thoughts are bothering them at night. If they are worrying about something specific at night, you could see if it would help to problem-solve the worry together (see page 127) or encourage them to seek professional support.
- Try to encourage them to sleep only at night, rather than recouping sleep by napping in the day. Sleeping in the day can make it harder to sleep again the next night and so exacerbate the problem.
- If you are sharing a bed with the person and this is impacting your sleep too, talk about this gently together to find solutions. This may mean having to sleep in different rooms, or problem-solving ways not to disturb each other once asleep.

LACK OF SELF-CARE

Depression makes a person feel like they are not good enough, not worth anything, a failure. They may lose all their energy, motivation and enthusiasm to care for themselves or care about their life. Personal care, washing and cleaning can all be affected. As a general rule, the more severe the depression, the more this can affect a person.

HOW TO HELP

- Remember R.E.L.A.T.E (see page 155).
- Be gentle, open and honest. Tell the person that you are worried about them, that you've noticed it looks like they might be struggling with taking care of themselves and their home. Acknowledge how hard things must be feeling for them. Be kind and gentle when you say this – no judgement, no blame, no criticism; just concern, empathy and support.
- With permission, talk together about how having a wash, tidying up etc. might make them feel better.
- With permission, see if you can help them. For example, run a bath for them, give them their toothbrush, do some washing, tidy a room together. Do a little bit at a time or as much as they feel able to do.
- If possible, do things together as it can help the person with depression if they feel engaged in the action too. It doesn't matter if you do more than them; if they can do a little, that is great.
- Aim for supporting them to do a little bit more each day.

CANCELLING PLANS

"If the person cancels, it is not because they don't care, but because the depression has become too big and overwhelming."

Depression makes a person feel overwhelmed by going out, with social activity, with facing other people. Depression can tell a person all the things that may go wrong if they go out, how they will be perceived or judged, or it will make them feel they have no energy to go out. It can make a person feel insecure, anxious, panicked, sad. It can feel physically, emotionally and cognitively overwhelming.

When depression is present, its heaviness ebbs and flows, just like the weather, some moments feeling easier than others. Understanding this is important because it helps explain why a person may say yes to plans at a time when the depression may feel less heavy, when the clouds have parted, but then when the depression descends again, they may feel less confident, more anxious or exhausted and unable to follow through on plans agreed.

HOW TO HELP
- Remember R.E.L.A.T.E (see page 155).
- If this is repeated behaviour, you might need to draw on

your own resources to manage your initial responses, if you feel irritated, frustrated and hopeless about plans being cancelled again. You need to make space to acknowledge for yourself how you feel and be kind to yourself about it. Direct your frustration at the depression, not at the person themselves.

- Remember that if the person is cancelling, it is not because of you, or because they don't care, but because the depression has become too big and overwhelming and is making them feel it is impossible to continue.

- Remember the depression can be like a constant negative voice telling the person repeatedly why they can't cope with or face a situation. It may be feeling unbearable for them at this time.

- You need to tread the balance of seeing if the person could be encouraged to change their mind and attend, versus being respectful of what they want in that moment (to withdraw).

- See if you can gently open up the conversation about how they are feeling about the activity, and what is making them feel they need to cancel.

- Explain that you would love them to be there, but you can hear how hard it feels to think about attending.

- See if there are ways to make the activity easier to attend – for example, meeting them to travel to the event; driving so you can get there and back quickly; choosing to attend only one part; agreeing how to support them when they are there etc. You could explore this in detail or ask, 'Is there anything I can do to make it easier, as I'd love you to be able to come?'

- If, despite these conversations, the person does not feel able to attend, respect this, gently, kindly and without judgement. Remember the depression will make them very sensitive to any criticism. They will already feel like a disappointment/failure and it is important not to add to this feeling.
- Let them know you understand, that you will miss them and you love them.
- Agree to check in again after the event to see how they are.
- If this behaviour happens repeatedly, and the person's depression is growing, you may want to start a conversation at another time, when there are no immediate social plans being discussed. You can gently and kindly talk about the pattern that is happening, and let them know you are worried and how it seems like things are feeling more difficult and the depression is getting stronger and making attending things harder and harder. See if you can have a conversation together to think about how you can tackle it. See Chapter 9 for practical ways to increase activity.

"Direct your frustration at the depression,
not at the person themselves."

DOING TOO MUCH

Some people, particularly those at the milder end of the depression spectrum, may still be functioning, working, parenting, socializing, volunteering, keeping going, doing everything themselves. However, they may be struggling, weighed down by everything the depression sends – the negative thoughts, the rollercoaster of negative emotions, the physical lethargy. But they keep going anyway, likely in part because the depression is sending them a negative narrative that pushes them to feel they must do more. For people who are functioning in this way, you will notice the exhaustion, the sadness, the worry, the stress, the irritability, the sensitivities, the struggling to keep up. What they actually most likely need is to stop, to pause, to rest, to take some time off, to allow others to help, to have a break, to look after themselves, to talk, to acknowledge what is going on and that they need to take care of themselves and let others take care of them.

HOW TO HELP
- Remember R.E.L.A.T.E (see page 155).
- Find a time to talk, over a coffee, a drink or a walk. Offer to cook them dinner. Make yourself available to talk. If meeting is tricky, text and phone instead.

- Encourage them to talk about themselves and how they are doing.
- If they respond with, 'I'm fine' and you feel they are avoiding, deflecting, changing the subject, or minimizing things, gently guide them back. Ask them, 'But, really, truly, how are you?' Don't accept 'I'm fine' without asking more.
- Be gentle, open and honest about what you are noticing. Let them know you are worried about them, that you can see how difficult things seem and that you want to help. Put into words for them what perhaps they cannot: 'This seems like it is too much. You are holding too much on your shoulders; this is too much for one person. You deserve to rest, support, let me/us/others help you. You deserve that.'
- See if you can help them acknowledge that things are difficult. They may or may not be ready to acknowledge this. This conversation may take several days/weeks. That's OK, it may be part of the process. Be gentle, be understanding. Don't push this. Be supportive wherever they are at. They will get there with time. Also, just saying: 'This isn't OK, you're dealing with a lot, I'm worried about you,' may be enough for now. It may make all the difference.
- If the person with depression can acknowledge things are difficult, see if you can open up the conversation about

how to help. Is there something they can do, or you can do, that might help, that might make a difference? What would they most need or want? Is there anything that they can pause or where others can help, such as with children or chores? Is there a way they could take time off work? Find time to exercise, to shop, to have a rest? See if you can agree a plan or find something that they could try. Perhaps they will accept your help or try to reach out to someone else. Be gentle with this. Go at their pace. It may take time for them. With permission, suggest a couple of ideas gently, but don't be surprised if they don't go for this straight away. It may take time for them to be ready to accept help and support and be willing to slow down.

"The depression is sending them a negative narrative that pushes them to feel they must do more."

- If the person with depression cannot envisage any way of stopping or slowing down, see if you can problem-solve any small things that could help, or that would be nice to plan in. Again, this may take time and several conversations.
- If you are having these conversations and you can see the depression may be worsening and the person's ability to cope seems to be reducing further, you may want to step

up the level of this conversation. Don't be afraid to say that you are worried about them, that you are worried things will feel worse if they don't find some time to rest and allow others to help. Continue to be gentle and compassionate and know that it may take some time for anything to change. Don't take it personally if they don't make changes immediately or if they don't follow your advice. This is a process. What is most important is that they know you provide a non-judgemental space where they can find support.

STUCK IN A CYCLE OF NEGATIVE THOUGHTS

Depression causes significant and intrusive levels of negative thoughts, such as 'I am a failure', 'I am useless', 'I am not good enough', 'I am broken' or 'I am worthless.' It also includes thoughts about others: 'Everyone else is able to do X. People must all think X about me' and thoughts about the future: 'Nothing good will happen', 'I can only see darkness', 'I can't imagine the future', ' Bad things will happen.'

It can be like a horse wearing blinkers, where the person can only see one aspect of a situation – the negative perspective. It is as if all their thoughts pass through a dark filter, a filter that skews the thoughts toward the worst case, the most negative conclusion, the darkest interpretation of themselves, or the situation. It is often a constant onslaught from the moment a person wakes up.

HOW TO HELP

- Remember R.E.L.A.T.E (see page 155).
- Keep in mind what it must be like for the person to have these negative thoughts.
- Keep in mind that the depression will be looking for every opportunity to jump on a word, a phrase or an action from you or others, that can be interpreted in a negative light.
- Keep in mind that when a person is struggling, responding differently, withdrawing etc. there is likely to be a running commentary in their mind, telling them how terrible, undeserving and unloved they are.
- Be kind, be supportive, tell them they are loved, missed, wanted. You can be a light; a warm, positive voice in the darkness.
- It is important to let them talk and tell you about the negative thoughts, so you can understand how the depression is talking to them. You may notice themes or patterns in what they say, with the same negative thoughts coming up again and again.
- Highlight that these negative thoughts are coming from the depression. 'I can hear that the depression is being really unkind to you/saying some really mean things/being

such a bully to you today.' 'Gosh I can hear how awful and critical the depression is being to you today.'

- Don't be afraid to talk about 'the depression'; to say things like:
  - o 'I would love you to come to X, but I can imagine the depression is probably telling you that you can't for some reason.'
  - o 'I think you are amazing, but I can understand it must be hard when the depression is telling you that you are failing.'
  - o 'I'm so sorry, it must be so hard when the depression is telling you all these terrible things about yourself.'
- Encourage kindness and self-compassion as an antidote to the depression. You can say: 'I can hear the depression is making you so critical toward yourself. Can you think about something kind you could say to yourself? Could you remind yourself you are struggling with depression and this is really hard, and so you are doing the best you can to get through this each day?' Let them know that until they feel able to be kind to themselves, you will send kindness and compassion their way for them. You can say something like: 'I hate to hear how the depression is talking to you/making you feel about yourself. I wish I could help you be kind

to yourself. You are doing the best you can in really difficult circumstances no matter what the depression tells you.'

- Understand that you may hear about these negative thoughts over and over again. Depression can be relentless, repetitive, ruminative. It can be difficult for the person to escape the critical thoughts. You may need to be kind and reassuring over and over again. Remember this can be very hard work, so be sure to take time out to look after yourself too (see Chapter 12).

- Understand that saying to someone, 'Don't be silly, of course that's not true' is not going to make them think differently. It may, in fact, make them feel unheard, like no one is listening.

- These principles, drawn from the Cognitive Behavioural Therapy (CBT) and Acceptance and Commitment Therapy (ACT) models (see pages 184 and 185) may be useful to keep in mind:

  o We cannot control which thoughts come into our mind.

  o Thoughts are not facts – just because we have them, doesn't mean they are true.

  o Thoughts in depression have often come through a negative filter and are biased toward the negative, with thinking errors common.

o Thinking errors can include black-and-white thinking (everything all good or all bad), catastrophizing (thinking about the worst-case scenario) or emotional reasoning ('Because I feel this it must be true'). Recognizing these can be helpful.

o Depression can hook a person into being completely fused together with their thoughts, and into listening to them, believing them and behaving differently because of this.

o With support, we can learn how to challenge our thoughts to create more rational or evidence-based thoughts, or to unhook and not be pushed around by them.

o With support, we can stop them having power over us or pushing us around.

o Therapy interventions can help a person learn strategies for this. You and the person with depression could also read more about CBT or ACT (see Resources).

"You can be a light – a warm, positive voice in the darkness."

• Tell them, or send them this message: 'If all you did today is put a hand on your heart and tell yourself you are loved, and you are going to get through this and be OK, then that is enough.'

IDENTIFYING THE NEED FOR PROFESSIONAL HELP

At the milder end of the depression spectrum (see page 8), seeking professional help (see Chapter 11) can prevent the depression spiralling further. The person may be more receptive to professional help at a time when the depression isn't so heavy (they may, however, also be less likely to be receptive to help as they may not feel their issues are 'bad enough' to warrant this). At the other end of the spectrum, where there is severe depression which is all-consuming and heavy, seeking help is so important as it may be hard for the person to come out of the severity of the depression without professional support.

HOW TO HELP

- Remember R.E.L.A.T.E (see page 155).
- Encourage an open and honest conversation about seeking professional help.
- Gently ask them if they have considered talking to someone (e.g. counselling/therapy) or if medication could help (more on this in Chapter 11).
- Be open to understanding that your views and beliefs about therapy and medication may be different to the person you are helping, and that what you would want may be different. Tread gently and, whilst you can share your views, don't impose them.

- If you feel very 'anti' any particular approach, it can be better to keep this to yourself as it is important that the person with depression feels able to access any support they feel ready for or that is advised/supported by a professional, without feeling that they will let you down or that you will disapprove.

- Encourage them to speak to a family doctor or other trusted health professional for help. See Chapter 11 for more details on this.

CHAPTER 11

PROFESSIONAL SUPPORT

Supporting a person with depression can be lonely, overwhelming and difficult. One of the most important things to remember is: you do not have to do this alone. You do not have to be, and *cannot be*, solely responsible for the person's wellbeing and recovery. You cannot be the only one checking in, nor the only one they can contact. There are some amazing resources, professionals and places to find support, if you know what you need and where to look.

This chapter will signpost you to where you can find support for the person you are helping, and of course for yourself too if you need it.

DIFFERENT ROUTES TO FIND SUPPORT

There are various levels of support and what is available may vary to some extent depending on the structure of public or private health services in your area. The routes include:

- Psychoeducation/self-help – information and self-help literature, books, websites and podcasts about depression (see Resources)
- Professional support – public sectors
- Professional support – private sectors
- Charity services, including crisis/support helplines
- Local community activities

PSYCHOEDUCATION

Psychoeducation means any information that may help someone understand what they may be experiencing and why, and how to help.

For the person with depression, and for yourself, knowing the signs and symptoms, and what to do when you experience them, can be extremely useful. Such knowledge and understanding can provide a sense of relief, making you more aware of what you are facing and feeling more empowered.

The aim of this book is to be a psychoeducational resource, and in Resources you will find a list of books, websites, podcasts and links for you to build your own additional resources.

THERAPY PROFESSIONALS

There are many different professionals you may meet or seek out, including:

Family doctor or GP: They usually have a general understanding of mental health difficulties and are helpful in diagnosis, medication and signposting toward specialist and therapeutic interventions where this is needed.

Psychiatric or mental health nurse: These specialist nurses support people with mental health difficulties with diagnosis, managing medication and working toward goals for recovery. They often work in teams or hospitals with other professionals.

Psychiatrist: A medical doctor who has completed specialist training in mental health, and the diagnosis of mental health difficulties or illnesses. Some psychiatrists will also have extra qualifications and training in therapy. A psychiatrist is qualified to prescribe psychiatric medication for mental health disorders/illnesses.

Psychological therapy professionals: There are a number of different professionals who offer psychological therapy or therapy-based interventions. I have provided some examples here.

- **Counsellor:** A counsellor will have completed a counselling-based qualification. A counselling session provides the space to talk about events in a person's life and how they are feeling. The counsellor provides non-judgemental empathic support.

o **Clinical psychologist**: A clinical psychologist will have completed a Doctoral level qualification in clinical psychology and are trained in assessment (including risk assessment), formulation, and a range of therapy approaches (e.g. ACT, CBT, Systemic, Psychodynamic, EMDR). They offer structured active therapy which – alongside providing a safe therapeutic space for a person to talk about and explore their difficulties – will also have a focus on the goals a person would like to achieve and the interventions, strategies or practical approaches that can be put in place to help both in-session and in-between sessions.

o **Counselling psychologist**: A counselling psychologist will have Doctoral level training (previously a Masters and practitioner diploma) in counselling psychology. Counselling psychologists are trained to understand and work with relationship dynamics and to use these to help a person understand themselves and how they interact with the world around them. As with clinical psychologists they provide assessment, formulation and evidence-based therapy interventions drawing on a range of models and approaches.

Please Note: There are a range of different professionals offering psychological interventions. Each professional will each have their specific skills and experiences that they have developed through their core training course and any additional training they have individually chosen to undertake. There is no one set description and what people offer will vary. Always look at a person's qualifications and particularly the recognized therapy/training they have completed and check that they are accredited or registered with a professional body. If a professional has completed recognized qualifications and is registered/accredited, it is usually displayed clearly on their websites or literature, or can be provided if requested.

CONFIDENTIALITY

Anything discussed at appointments with mental health professionals will be confidential to the person (within the limits of confidentiality related to managing risk where the professional may have to liaise with other professionals to manage risk). If information has to be shared with any other professional in the person's support system, such as the family doctor, it will be discussed with the patient first. The mental health professional will be bound to maintain confidentiality, so will not be able to enter into any discussion with you, as a supporter, unless the person you are helping has given explicit consent.

PSYCHOLOGICAL INTERVENTIONS AND TYPES OF THERAPY

There are a number of different psychological interventions and therapy approaches. I have described some common approaches here.

COUNSELLING APPROACHES

Counselling focuses on talking about and understanding yourself and others and helping you find ways forward, without typically giving specific advice. Approaches can include humanistic counselling or integrative counselling.[5]

COGNITIVE BEHAVIOURAL THERAPY (CBT)

CBT is an active talking therapy. It is goal-orientated and often involves completing tasks or 'homework' in-between sessions, as agreed with the client and therapist (hence the active description). CBT looks at the interaction between the environment we are in and how we think and feel, the physical symptoms we experience and how we behave. It identifies the impact of early experience and the core beliefs that a person may hold, which influences how they think and feel about themselves, others and the world. CBT is a widely used well-researched therapy approach for people with depression.

There is also mindfulness-based cognitive therapy which incorporates elements of CBT and mindfulness approaches into the therapy.

ACCEPTANCE AND COMMITMENT THERAPY (ACT)

ACT focuses on supporting a person to acknowledge and accept that difficult thoughts and feelings may show up, and that they can notice these, make space for these, manage these, and find ways to take action despite these difficult experiences being present. ACT incorporates techniques from mindfulness, helps a person be in the present moment, defuse from the intensity of their thoughts and take committed action toward a meaningful life in the choices they make every day. ACT has a number of useful tools and strategies that help a person with depression.

COMPASSION FOCUSED THERAPY (CFT)

Compassion-focused therapy draws on the benefits of being able to be compassionate, and to develop the ability to feel soothed, safe and warm in a person's interactions with themselves and others – and especially, to be self-compassionate. CFT was initially developed to help people with shame and self-criticism and so is well suited for people experiencing depression.

EYE MOVEMENT DESENSITIZATION REPROCESSING (EMDR)

EMDR is a therapy approach that was initially developed for trauma and post-traumatic stress disorder (PTSD). However, it has been developed to treat a range of mental health difficulties, including depression, anxiety, grief and phobias. It involves processing memories, thoughts, feelings and sensations in sessions using specific EMDR protocols.

PSYCHODYNAMIC OR PSYCHOANALYTIC PSYCHOTHERAPIES

Psychodynamic or psychoanalytic psychotherapies are a long-term, more intensive and in-depth therapy approach. They draw on the understanding of unconscious processes, internal conflicts, and relationship dynamics. Often sessions are once or twice weekly and can be offered over a period of years. Shorter-term psychodynamic or psychoanalytic therapies have also been developed, for example cognitive analytic therapy (CAT).

SYSTEMIC/COUPLES THERAPY/ NARRATIVE THERAPY

Systemic therapies focus on understanding theories and approaches related to systems, family dynamics and relationships rather than focusing just on the individual. For a person with depression there may be times when family therapy can be useful, if relationship dynamics are contributing to the depression.

MEDICATION

Medical doctors, psychiatric nurses and psychiatrists can prescribe medication. For depression there are a number of different types of medications that can be tried, for example, for low mood, anxiety, sleep or agitation.

As a clinical psychologist my focus is on psychological and therapy approaches. I am not trained in prescribing medication. Therefore, I would always advise you to talk to an appropriately trained medical professional to find out more about medication.

What I can tell you is that I frequently work with people who access therapy and take medication, or who choose one route or the other (e.g. only therapy or only medication). For those who take medication, some only require this for a short period of time, and some take this for longer. What is important, should a person choose medication, is to take it regularly and consistently in line with the instructions for it to be most effective.

I believe the decision to take medication, as with all other interventions, should be an individual and informed choice after speaking with appropriately qualified professionals (and based on the individual circumstances, symptoms, approaches previously tried and personal choices/beliefs).

CHOOSING THE RIGHT SUPPORT

The support needed will vary depending on what the person may be ready for or need, due to the severity of the depression.

When depression is mild, the person may be able to support themselves without intervention, but they may also find that talking to the family doctor and accessing counselling/therapy and/or medication is helpful.

When depression becomes moderate to severe, it may be that more professional support is required including seeing the family doctor, accessing therapeutic interventions, psychiatry input and medication – and the support of a mental health team or hospital admission may be required. What may be needed will vary. Everyone is individual.

There are times when the depression becomes very severe and the risk becomes high, so that the person, for their own safety, may urgently need support or an admission to hospital. If a person is too ill to consent to this (and are assessed to lack capacity under mental capacity laws), mental health professionals may have to apply mental health legislation to seek an admission without a person's consent often known as 'sectioning'. This can be an upsetting time for you and the person with depression and if you are in this situation it is important that you both have as much support as you can access.

FINDING AND ACCESSING SUPPORT

The structure of accessing mental health support can vary depending on where you live and what is available in your area. It can vary in terms of what is available through the government or state-run mental health systems and what is available privately. Below is a summary of what you may expect in each area.

PROFESSIONAL SUPPORT IN THE PUBLIC SECTOR

Often the first place to seek support is by having an appointment with the family doctor/GP, who may be able to refer you or help you access further services.

Local public health services may include access to specialist professionals (psychologists, counsellors, psychiatrists), and also to specialist services, for example, mental health teams for adults, young people, or older people, or teams for people with learning disabilities, physical health or chronic pain problems, or with specific conditions such as trauma or postnatal/postpartum depression.

Many public health services now also have their own websites and helplines where you can find out more about what they offer.

PROFESSIONAL SUPPORT IN THE PRIVATE SECTOR

In the private sector you will find a range of professionals working privately such as private doctors, counsellors and clinical/counselling psychologists, private psychiatrists, private mental health hospitals and, in some instances, private community mental health teams.

There is a cost to private treatment or interventions and the person with depression will need to fund this themselves or have someone fund it for them.

In some areas, private health insurance can cover the cost of mental health support and it is worth checking if the person with depression has this or is covered by a policy.

CHARITIES AND HELPLINES

There are some fantastic places to find support in the charity sector and online or via text or phone services. For the person struggling with depression and for yourself as a helper, it is important to know there are places to find support.

There are mental health organizations that offer support and information via their websites, and in some cases they also offer phone support or text lines, as well as support groups that people can attend in person or virtually. Please see Resources for more information on this.

COMMUNITY ACTIVITIES

As awareness of mental health has grown and we have become more aware of the benefits of social engagement, exercise and activity in supporting mental health, so have initiatives developed that provide opportunities for people struggling with their mental health.

For a person with depression, the opportunity to get outside and be active and around other people can be invaluable. Depending on your area, there may be different things on offer. Examples include walking sessions for people with mental health difficulties; gardening sessions; coffee mornings; exercise.

You can check with your family doctor, library, community centre or local mental health organizations to find out about possible activities on offer in your area.

"For a person with depression, the opportunity to get outside and be active and around other people can be invaluable."

WHEN SUPPORT ISN'T THERE

Sadly, there may be times when you or the person with depression reaches out and the support isn't there. Perhaps waiting lists are long or interventions limited; perhaps the person you speak to isn't very helpful or accommodating; perhaps the funds aren't there, or a referral gets lost... and so on. The reality is that sometimes reaching out doesn't go perfectly. I know this, and I see it and hear it from the people I work with and in my personal life. However, all I can say is: please, don't give up. There are some incredible people and resources out there. There are some brilliant books, podcasts, free resources and helplines. There are some wonderful practitioners who want to help. If you know help is needed, keep exploring all the different options set out here and I hope you find the right help and support you and the person with depression deserve.

CHAPTER 12

YOUR OWN SELF-CARE

Before I begin this chapter, I want to thank you for being willing to keep going and for helping someone with depression, even when it feels tough. It isn't easy. It takes a lot of your own emotional, physical and cognitive resources to offer support. This is what depression does, what it takes from the person experiencing depression and those around them. Thank you for everything you have offered to the person you are supporting so far.

This chapter is about you looking after yourself, so that you can stay well and offer ongoing support without being overwhelmed by the heaviness and hopelessness of the depression.

Whilst this chapter is for you, you might want to gently share some of the ideas in it with the person you are helping, given that self-care is often completely lost when depression takes over.

'PUT YOUR OWN OXYGEN MASK ON FIRST'

When you travel by plane, the safety instructions always include: 'Put your own oxygen mask on before you help others' – you have to first look after yourself. Well, self-care is a little like that. So here are four important reasons why you need self-care:

1. Studies have shown that people who take on a role caring or supporting others can have their own emotional and physical wellbeing impacted. Supporting someone with depression can weigh heavily on your emotions, your physical resources and your thoughts. It can occupy your mind, affect how you feel, leave you feeling exhausted, worried, drained, hopeless, frustrated and overwhelmed. Ultimately, if you become exhausted, burnt out and experience mental health struggles yourself, this will not be good for you or the person you are supporting, or any others who are part of your life. So being able to use self-care tools to cope and to look after yourself, and enhance your wellbeing, is not just helpful, but essential.

2. Research has shown that engaging in self-care activities reduces burnout, improves sleep, increases energy, reduces compassion fatigue (see page 103), prevents you depleting your coping resources, improves your immune

system, and boosts productivity and effectiveness (which in this context, is your ability to be a supporter and function in daily life).

3. Everyone deserves and should have self-care as part of their daily life. Regardless of your role as a supporter for someone with depression, self-care will enhance your mental health and wellbeing and enable you to feel as mentally well as possible. Just for you. Because you are important.

> "Self-care is not an indulgence. It is an essential... it should not be considered as something 'extra' or 'nice to do if you have the time'."[6]

4. Self-care isn't selfish. It is essential to your wellbeing and if you practise self-care, you will be more effective and more able to help, support and care for people around you. To be able to function day to day, do your job, to parent. By practising good self-care, you are also modelling to others how important and OK it is to take care of yourself. So, if not for yourself, remember that practising self-care helps everyone around you.

WHAT EXACTLY IS SELF-CARE?

Self-care is anything that makes you feel good, that helps recharge you, soothe you, calm you, energize you; and that leaves you feeling refreshed, rested and mentally well.

It can be anything from giving yourself permission to rest, practising a breathing exercise, going for a run, allowing yourself to have the night off from working/chores, or going to therapy. You'll find lots more ideas for self-care in the next few pages.

Sometimes the term self-care can be a bit off putting. It's become a bit of a cliché phrase, an overly used term, but it's meaning is so important. We could also call it: looking after

---

SELF-CARE

S   Soothes you

E   Re-Energizes you

L   Lifts you up

F   Feeds your soul

C   Care and compassion for you

A   Acknowledges you are important

R   Helps you Rest and sleep

E   Empowers you to cope

---

yourself; doing something to make you feel good; finding ways to rest and recharge; doing something kind for yourself. It's like taking your car for a service to help it run smoothly. However you want to describe it, let's make sure you have some of this in your life.

"Self-care is for everyone. *Everyone* deserves and benefits from self-care."

HANG ON, THAT'S NOT SELF-CARE!

There will be ideas in this chapter that might make you think 'That's not self-care!' For example, 'tidying the bedroom'. Yet you'll read this here, because, in some circumstances, prioritizing tidying the bedroom so that you have a calm, soothing space to sleep in might be a really important act of self-care. It's all about balance and figuring out what will be right for you in that moment.

I REALLY DON'T HAVE TIME FOR SELF-CARE

After you've read through this chapter, I hope you will be surprised at all the ways self-care can be part of your life. And, yes, self-care means dedicating time and energy in a meaningful way to these activities. But it can also mean finding five minutes, even one minute, in your day for a self-care activity. And hopefully this chapter will help you feel it is possible to find this time, and, more importantly, help you think: 'Can I really afford *not* to make time for this?'

DIFFERENT TYPES OF SELF-CARE

Ultimately self-care can be *anything* that helps you feel calmed, soothed, recharged, re-energized and rested; that helps you feel care and compassion toward yourself. There are different ways we can categorize self-care, including:

- Physical self-care
- Emotional self-care
- Spiritual self-care
- Mental self-care
- Social self-care
- Practical self-care

Here are some further ways of thinking about self-care:

- **Looking after yourself:** The basic building blocks of self-care (e.g. washing, brushing teeth, cleaning, feeding yourself) can often fall by the wayside when we prioritize others.

- **Health and fitness:** This can be anything that involves taking care of what you put into your body – good nutrition – as well as moving your body in enjoyable ways. We know that both these elements can enhance our wellbeing and improve mental and physical health. Exercise, in whatever form works for you, is a vital element of maintaining good mental health, as it is known to improve mood, decision-making, problem-solving, memory, self-esteem, self-confidence and more.

- **Fresh air and nature:** Any activities that encourage getting outside, amongst nature, with access to natural light have been found to enhance wellbeing and lift mood.

- **Getting tasks done:** Sometimes self-care is about prioritizing getting tasks done. Whether it is doing housework so you have a tidy house to relax in, or doing laundry so you have fresh bedding, or decluttering, organizing, or paying bills, or completing a task you've been putting off. Sometimes doing these tasks adds to a sense of being able to relax and rest, which is a good thing. There is always a fine line with these tasks, however – if doing them adds to stress or exhaustion, then it isn't self-care.

- **Being in the moment:** Being able to use breathing and grounding exercises can be incredibly helpful for quick self-care (see Resources). Being able to learn mindfulness skills and/or mindfulness meditation can bring more calm and sense of being present in the moment. Being able to learn and use relaxation and visualizations can help with rest and sleep. All of these are powerful and well-established means of helping calm, centre and ground you.

MINDFULNESS

Mindfulness is the ability at any given moment, to be in the present, to notice what is going on through the senses (what you can see, hear, touch, taste or smell) and in your mind, emotions and body.

Being able to be mindful can involve very practical mindfulness-based exercises that you can use in daily life, or it may be practising mindfulness meditations.

- **Spirituality:** Connecting with religion, prayer, or spiritual processes, behaviours or beliefs systems can be part of a healthy self-care routine for some people.
- **Social connection:** This includes any tasks that encourage social connection in a meaningful, positive way. It might

be a supportive text, a call, a video chat, a walk with a friend or family, a date... Social connection is so important to us as humans and can help us feel loved, important, cared for, part of a team and supported. It is a way to share stresses and care, and be cared for. As a helper, it is essential that you also have your own social network of support.

- **Doing things that makes you smile:** Anything that brings you joy and pleasure is important for self-care.
- **Being kind to yourself:** Anything that encourages self-compassion, including speaking kindly to yourself, treating yourself, setting boundaries, knowing when to say no, giving yourself permission to rest, and more.
- **Seeking or accepting support:** Allowing yourself to be supported is also a form of self-care – reaching out when you need help and accepting it when it is offered. This might be support from your family and friends, or from mental health professionals.

SELF-CARE IDEAS

Sometimes, even when you have made time for self-care, it can be hard to think of specific ideas, especially when you are exhausted. So, I have created a list of self-care ideas (not exhaustive), rather like a menu, that you can choose from. Read through this list to see how many you would like to try, that you can imagine would help you feel a little more relaxed, soothed, recharged, re-energized, and that would help you feel ready to face the day again.

- Drink water
- Have a relaxing bath
- Wear your favourite clothes
- Cook something you love
- Go for a walk/run/jog/play a sport
- Move your body (stretch, dance, yoga)
- Have your morning cup of tea in the garden
- Visit a nature spot/park/sea/woods
- Get something done from your to-do list
- Make your bed and ensure your bedroom is a calm, peaceful place
- Organize clutter
- Tidy up a room in the house
- Do something you've been putting off
- Learn and practise some breathing exercises
- Learn and practise mindfulness meditation
- Listen to your favourite music
- Turn your phone off
- Have a day off social media

- Spend time in a religious or spiritual activity that is meaningful for you
- Journal
- Connect with friends/family/your partner
- Go on a date
- Get a hug from a loved one
- Do something that makes you laugh
- Do something creative – paint, draw, dance
- Take up a new hobby – photography, art, dance, Lego, anything!
- Read a book
- Meet your own sexual needs
- Watch your favourite movie or TV show
- Cuddle a pet
- Play your favourite music in the shower
- Give yourself permission to take time off – an hour, an evening, a day, a weekend, a week
- Have boundaries – and implement them
- Practise self-compassion
- Buy yourself some flowers
- Ask for help
- Accept help when offered
- See a therapist

For further ideas for self-care activities including breathing exercises, mindfulness exercises, mindful walking, self-compassion and grounding exercises, you will find a selection of resources on my website: www.empowerpsychology.co.uk

YOUR HELPER'S CHECKLIST

Helping someone overcome depression as a supporter is multi-faceted. Looking at the experience from all angles and considering how you can help through a range of approaches and strategies is likely to be most effective. We have covered a range of ways of helping within the book, and you have built your knowledge and toolkit of strategies for helping someone with depression.

As we reach the end of our journey in this book I have set out a checklist for you to use to cover off the different ways you can help. The checklist includes the main ideas we have covered in this book.

You could support someone with depression using as many of these as you feel able, or help the person seek support for these also (via other parts of the support system – family/friends or professionals); whilst also acknowledging you may not be able to, and do not have to, hold responsibility for supporting everything on this list:

- Talk to the person about identifying that this is depression.
- Offer kindness, compassion and empathy.
- Keep communicating, where possible using a person's preferred means.
- Be there to listen to the experience of depression and to support emotions.
- Explore any sleeping difficulties and ways to help improve sleep.
- Explore any eating difficulties and ways to encourage eating well.
- Explore practical ways to help with daily tasks, looking after themselves or the home.
- Look at ways to encourage increased movement, activity and exercise.
- Support getting outside regularly.
- Look at ways to increase pleasurable activities, activities that bring a sense of achievement and activities that encourage social connection.
- Encourage attendance at work or school, but also balance this with rest and slowing down when needed.
- Look at encouraging the reduction of avoidance and withdrawal behaviours.
- Talk about support options (e.g. speaking to the family doctor, therapy or medication).

- Encourage self-care in yourself and the person with depression.
- Don't be afraid to talk about risk, self-harm or suicide if you are worried about this.
- Seek your own help and support.
- Don't give up.

THE END – AND
THE BEGINNING

And so you have reached the end of this book. Thank you for reading.

I hope you have found new learning, new ideas, hope and inspiration amongst these pages and built your own supporter's toolkit along the way. I hope that you feel energized with ideas and ways you can help and with a new awareness and understanding. I hope, if you were feeling compassion fatigue sweeping in before, that this has helped you steady yourself and find your way to a place where you can look after yourself and offer support in a way that feels good for you and for the person you are helping.

Whilst this is the end, this is also the beginning. It is the beginning of a new chapter in your journey as a helper. A time to choose a fresh path, with your new ideas and strategies and understanding, to help yourself and the person you are supporting keep moving forward as they gently find their way through the depression.

I wish you all the love and support on your journey.

ACKNOWLEDGEMENTS

I am so grateful for the support and encouragement I have received in writing this book. I want to thank Beth Bishop for her kind support, guidance and faith in me and my writing. I am grateful to my wonderful colleagues, Gaby and Clare, who took their time to read early drafts, Tara for her helpful advice, as well as my ever-supportive parents, sister, and wonderful friends Ruth and Emma, who all kindly gave their time in one way or another. I am thankful to my family and friends, and my two wonderful boys who have patiently encouraged and supported me, and allowed me time to write through this whole process. And I am ever inspired by the incredible people with depression and supporters of someone with depression whom I have worked with, who have taught me so much and those who have shared their words and stories in this book. Thank you, all of you.

ENDNOTES

1   British Psychological Society (2020), *Understanding Depression: Why adults experience depression and what can help*. Retrieved April 2021 from www.bps.org.uk/sites/www.bps.org.uk/files/Member%20Networks/Divisions/DCP/Understanding%20depression.pdf

2   British Psychological Society and the Division of Clinical Psychology. *Understanding psychiatric diagnosis in adult mental health*. Retrieved April 2021 from www.bps.org.uk/sites/www.bps.org.uk/files/Member%20Networks/Divisions/DCP/Understanding%20psychiatric%20diagnosis%20in%20adult%20mental%20health.pdf

3   www.thecalmzone.net

4   *Suicides in England and Wales 2019 registrations*, Office for National Statistics. Accessed April 2021 from www.ons.gov.uk/peoplepopulationandcommunity/birthsdeathsandmarriages/deaths/bulletins/suicidesintheunitedkingdom/2019registrations

5   Counselling is sometimes used as a generic/colloquial term for therapy, but it is also a specific approach, separate to other types of therapy approaches.

6   Barnett, J. E., Johnston, L. C., & Hillard,
    D. (2006). Psychotherapist wellness as an
    ethical imperative. In L. VandeCreek & J. B.
    Allen (Eds.), *Innovations in clinical practice: Focus on
    health and wellness* p2630. Sarasota, FL: Professional
    Resources Press

RESOURCES

If you wish to explore further sources for reading, learning and understanding, I have put together a list of resources for you and for the person with depression. This is by no means an exhaustive list, but a jumping-off point to further your reading.

I have also created a number of freely accessible and downloadable resources which you will find on my website www.empowerpsychology.co.uk. This includes resources related to breathing and grounding exercises, sleep, self-care, mindfulness, mindful walking, wellbeing and more.

BOOKS
Books About Personal Experiences of Depression

Gordon, Bryony, *Mad Girl* (Headline, 2016)

Haig, Matt, *Reasons to Stay Alive* (Canongate, 2015)

Lawson, Jenny, *Furiously Happy: A funny book about horrible things* (Flatiron, 2015)

Mackie, Bella, *Jog On* (William Collins, 2019)

Reed, Charlotte, *My Path to Happy: Struggles with my mental health and all the wonderful things that happened after* (Andrews McMeel Publishing, 2020)

Sanders, Ali, *When the Bough Breaks* (Trigger, 2019)

Williams, Mark, *Daddy Blues* (Trigger, 2018)

Williams, Terrie M, *Black Pain: It just looks like we're not hurting* (Scribner, 2009)

Books About Ways to Help Depression

These include self-help books drawing on therapeutic approaches.

Gilbert, Paul, *Overcoming Depression: A self-help guide using cognitive behavioural techniques* (Robinson, 2009)

Williams, Chris, *Overcoming Depression and Low Mood: A five areas approach* (CRC Press, 2014)

Williams, Mark, *The Mindful Way through Depression: Freeing yourself from chronic unhappiness* (Guildford Press, 2007)

Williams, Chris, *Overcoming Postnatal Depression: A five areas approach* (Hodder Arnold, 2008)

Withy, James, *How to Tell Depression to Piss Off* (Robinson, 2020)

Books About Ways to Help Mental Health Issues Including Depression

These books draw on therapeutic techniques.

Beaumont, Elaine & Irons, Chris, *The Compassionate Mind Workbook* (Robinson, 2017)

Butler, Gillian, Grey, Nick & Hope, Tony, *Manage your Mind: The mental fitness guide* (OUP, 2007)

Guest, Jennifer, *The CBT Art Activity Book* (Jessica Kingsley, 2015)

Harris, Russ, *The Happiness Trap (ACT)* (Robinson, 2008)

Harris, Russ, *The Reality Slap (ACT)* (Robinson, 2021)

Pullen, William, *Run For Your Life: Mindful running for a happy life* (Penguin Life, 2018)

Walker, Rheeda, *The Unapologetic Guide to Black Mental Health* (New Harbinger, 2020)

Williams, Mark, *Mindfulness: A practical guide to finding peace in a frantic world* (Piatkus, 2011)

Books about Wellbeing, Self-Care or to Inspire

Chatterjee, Dr Rangan, *The Four Pillar Plan* (Penguin, 2017)

Curtis, Scarlett, *It's Not OK to Feel Blue (and Other Lies)* (Penguin, 2020)

Novogratz, Sukey, & Novogratz, Elizabeth, *Just Sit: A meditation guidebook for people who know they should but don't* (Harper Wave, 2017)

Macksey, Charlie, *The Boy the Fox and the Mole* (Ebury, 2019)

Reading, Suzy, *Self-care for Tough Times* (Aster, 2021)

Reading, Suzy, *The Self-care Revolution* (Aster, 2017)

Wax, Ruby, *How to be Human* (Penguin Life, 2018)

Weintraub, Amy, *Yoga for Depression* (Broadway Books, 2003)

Books for Children and Young People

Gilbert Bedia, Elizabeth, *Arthur wants a balloon* (Trigger, 2020)

Reading, Suzy, *Stand Tall Like a Mountain* (Aster, 2019)

Schab, Lisa M, *Beyond the Blues: A workbook to help teens overcome depression* (New Harbinger, 2008)

Sedley, Ben, *Stuff that Sucks* (Instant Help, 2017)

Spence, Dr Ruth, *Charlie and the Dog who Came to Stay* (Cherish Editions, 2021)

The Happy Self Journal: www.happyselfjournal.com

GENERAL MENTAL HEALTH WEBSITES

The are many organizations and useful websites specific to different countries or areas. Please contact your local mental health services/library/community centre to find out about mental health organizations in your area.

UK

Anxiety UK: Helpline: 03444 775 774, www.anxietyuk.org.uk

Heads Together: www.headstogether.org.uk

Hub of Hope: hubofhope.co.uk

Mental Health Foundation UK: www.mentalhealth.org.uk

Mind UK: www.mind.org.uk

PANDAS (PND support): pandasfoundation.org.uk

Rethink Mental Illness: www.rethink.org

Samaritans: www.samaritans.org, helpline: 116 123

Scottish Association for Mental Health (SAMH) (Scotland): www.samh.org.uk

Shout: www.giveusashout.org, text 85258

Young Minds: www.youngminds.org.uk

USA

Anxiety & Depression Association of America: adaa.org

HelpGuide: www.helpguide.org

Mentalhealth.gov: www.mentalhealth.gov

Mental Health America: www.mhanational.org

National Alliance on Mental Illness (NAMI): www.nami.org

National Institute of Mental Health: www.nimh.nih.gov

Very Well Mind: www.verywellmind.com

Canada

Anxiety Canada: www.anxietycanada.com

Canadian Mental Health Association: cmha.ca

Crisis Service Canada: www.ementalhealth.ca

Australia and New Zealand

Anxiety New Zealand Trust: www.anxiety.org.nz

Beyond Blue: www.beyondblue.org.au

Head to Health: headtohealth.gov.au

Health Direct: www.healthdirect.gov.au

Mental Health Australia: mhaustralia.org

Mental Health Foundation of New Zealand:
www.mentalhealth.org.nz
SANE Australia: www.sane.org

SUPPORT FOR SUICIDAL THOUGHTS
Crisis Text Line (USA, Canada, Ireland, UK):
www.crisistextline.org

UK
Campaign Against Living Miserably (CALM):
www.thecalmzone.net
PAPYRUS (dedicated to the prevention of young suicide):
www.papyrus-uk.org
The Samaritans: www.samaritans.org helpline: 116 123

USA
American Foundation for Suicide Prevention: afsp.org
National Suicide Prevention Lifeline:
suicidepreventionlifeline.org

Canada
Canada Suicide Prevention Crisis Service:
www.crisisservicescanada.ca

Australia and New Zealand

Lifeline Australia: www.lifeline.org.au

Lifeline Aotearoa: www.lifeline.org.nz

DEPRESSION AND DIVERSITY

Black African and Asian Therapy Network: www.baatn.org.uk

Embrace Multicultural Mental Health:
www.embracementalhealth.org.au

The Institute for Muslim Mental Health
www.muslimmentalhealth.com/islam-mental-health

CARERS SUPPORT

Carers UK: www.carersuk.org

Family Carers Ireland: familycarers.ie

National Alliance for Caregiving (USA): caregiving.org

Carers Canada: carerscanada.ca

Carers Australia: carersaustralia.com.au

Carers New Zealand: carers.net.nz

PSYCHOLOGICAL SOCIETIES AND ASSOCIATIONS

British Psychological Society (UK): bps.org.uk

Royal College of Psychiatrists (UK): rcpsych.ac.uk

American Psychological Association: apa.org

Canadian Psychological Association: cpa.org

Australian Psychological Society: psychology.org.au

SELF-REPORT MEASURES

Freely available self-report measures for depression include:

- Anxiety and Depression Checklist (K10): www.beyondblue.org.au/the-facts/anxiety-and-depression-checklist-k10
- APA: Patient Health Questionnaire (PHQ-9): www.apa.org/depression-guideline/patient-health-questionnaire.pdf
- Geriatric Depression Scale: psychology-tools.com/geriatric-depression-scale

PODCASTS

A selection of podcasts about depression, mental health, wellbeing and therapy:

- Bryony Gordon's Mad World
- Feel Better, Live More: Dr Chatterjee
- Happy Place: Fearne Cotton
- Let's Talk about CBT: Dr Lucy Maddox
- Man Talk: Jamie Day
- Mental Health Foundation Podcasts
- People Soup: Ross McIntosh
- Psychologists off the Clock: Debbie Sorensen, Diana Hill, Yael Schonrbun
- Terrible, Thanks for Asking: Nora Mcireny

- Therapy for Black Girls: Joy Hayden Bradford
- Therapy Lab: Dr Sheri Jacobson

WELLBEING APPS

- Action for Happiness
- Calm
- Headspace
- Insight Timer
- Nourish
- Shine

OTHER RESOURCES

- Russ Harris (ACT) has a number of fantastic audio resources including the grounding exercise dropping anchor which can be found here: www.actmindfully.com.au/free-stuff/free-audio
- Dream Completion Technique by Dr Justin Havens is a useful video for managing bad dreams and nightmares: www.youtube.com/watch?v=lv38dzpcxfA

TriggerHub.org is one of the most elite and scientifically proven forms of mental health intervention

Trigger Publishing is the leading independent mental health and wellbeing publisher in the UK and US. Clinical and scientific research conducted by assistant professor Dr Kristin Kosyluk and her highly acclaimed team in the Department of Mental Health Law & Policy at the University of South Florida (USF), as well as complementary research by her peers across the US, has independently verified the power of lived experience as a core component in achieving mental health prosperity. Specifically, the lived experiences contained within our bibliotherapeutic books are intrinsic elements in reducing stigma, making those with poor mental health feel less alone, providing the privacy they need to heal, ensuring they know the essential steps to kick-start their own journeys to recovery, and providing hope and inspiration when they need it most.

Delivered through TriggerHub, our unique online portal and accompanying smartphone app, we make our library of bibliotherapeutic titles and other vital resources accessible to individuals and organizations anywhere, at any time and with complete privacy, a crucial element of recovery. As such, TriggerHub is the primary recommendation across the UK and US for the delivery of lived experiences.

At Trigger Publishing and TriggerHub, we proudly lead the way in making the unseen become seen. We are dedicated to humanizing mental health, breaking stigma and challenging outdated societal values to create real action and impact. Find out more about our world-leading work with lived experience and bibliotherapy via triggerhub. org, or by joining us on:

 @triggerhub_

 @triggerhub.org

 @triggerhub_